"Gregory Jantz is a man with a heart for those who agonize over their weight, and he has written a book to help us understand that successful weight loss goes beyond the mere issue of food and into the realm of our minds and emotions. He encourages us to ask ourselves deep questions so we can deal honestly with the past, realistically with the present, and expectantly with regard to the future."
—**Stormie Omartian,** author of several books including *Better Body Management* and *Greater health God's Way,* and the aerobic videos *Exercise for Life I & II*

"Dr. Jantz's whole-person approach to weight loss is an idea long overdue."
—**Denis Waitley,** Ph.D., author of many books, including *The Psychology of Winning,* and several tape series including the new 12-tape set *The Psychology of Living Lean*

"As a cardiologist and medical director of Stevens Weight Management Clinic, I find Jantz's book to be useful for everyone motivated towards permanent weight loss. Dr. Jantz presents a very readable workbook which involves the reader in specific exercises and assignments related to the psychological and spiritual aspects of permanent weight management."
—**Stephen Yarnall,** M.D., known as "Dr. Cookie" and coauthor of the *Dr. Cookie Cookbook*

"Fresh! Wonderful insights for the fight against fat."
—**Covert Bailey,** whose books such as *Fit or Fat* and *The New Fit or Fat* have sold over 3.5 million copies

D0965132

Losing Weight Permanently

LOSING WEIGHT
Permanently

SECRETS
OF THE
2%
WHO
SUCCEED

GREGORY L. JANTZ, PH.D.

Harold Shaw Publishers
Wheaton, Illinois

All Scripture quotations, unless otherwise indicated, are taken from *The Holy Bible: New International Version*. Copyright © 1973, 1978, 1984 by the International Bible Society. Used by permission of Zondervan Publishing House.

Story on pages 51-54 is taken from *Forgive and Forget* by Lewis B. Smedes. Copyright © 1984 by Lewis B. Smedes. Reprinted by permission of HarperCollins, Inc.

"A Child's Ten Commandments to Parents" on page 203 by Dr. Kevin Leman is used by permission of the author, who is also the author of *Making Children Mind without Losing Yours*.

ISBN 0-87788-480-3

Cover design by David LaPlaca

Library of Congress Cataloging-in-Publication Data

Jantz, Gregory L.
    Losing weight permanently : secrets of the 2% who succeed / Gregory L. Jantz.
      p.   cm.
    ISBN 0-87788-480-3
    1. Weight loss. I. Title.
  RM222.2.J37 1996
  613.2'5—dc20
                                              96-3837
                                                CIP

---

03 02 01 00 99 98 97 96

10 9 8 7 6 5 4 3 2 1

*To those, who are among the two percent,
who have stayed with their program of
permanent weight loss.
Thank you for teaching us so much through
your great success so that we may, in turn,
help others.*

CONTENTS

Acknowledgments...11

1 Free from the Tangles of Dieting..........................13

2 No More Sneak Attacks....................................29

3 Eating As an Art..51

4 The Dance of Sex and Weight.............................70

5 From Guilt Cycle to Bicycle..............................90

6 A Nutritional Plan That Really Works.................107

7 Developing Intimacy with People......................131

8 Eating Problems and Their Link to Abuse..........151

9 Maintain Membership in the 2 Percent Club......173

Appendix One
The Addiction Checklist..................................188

Appendix Two
Attention Deficit Disorder and Learning Disabilities:
Their Relationship to Overeating 191

Appendix Three
Raising Children to Resist Eating Problems.............199

ACKNOWLEDGMENTS

I would like to express my heartfelt thanks to the many individuals who have provided me with such invaluable insights and assistance by telling us their remarkable stories. But stories are simply stories without an editor, and Joan Guest has believed in this project from its inception. Without Joan's editorial skill and constant encouragement, this book may never have seen the light of day.

I owe a great debt of gratitude to my colaborer and project manager, Robert C. Larson, whose belief in the vision for this book helped make it a reality. Bob and I kept the phone lines humming and used many rolls of fax paper in working through this manuscript. I'm deeply indebted to him for both his organizational and writing skills. I would also like to thank my research assistants, LaFon Jantz and Jennifer Bodnar, Director of Seminars, who were always there when they were needed most. This brief thanks to them does not do their contribution justice, but it comes from a heart filled with gratitude. I would also like to acknowledge the supervisory staff at the Center for Counseling and Health Resources for their unfailing support of this project.

I especially salute Mike Weiford, M.S.W., Robert Anderson, M.D., Shelly Miller, M.A., Susan Blake, M.A., and Greg Bauer, C.D.C., for their encouragement, support, and participation in helping to form the content of this book, while also supporting the daily work of the Center. I am also grateful to my fellow colleagues who through the years have referred so many men, women, boys, and girls to our eating disorder program. You have supported us as we've worked with people who've walked through these remarkable journeys to permanent weight loss. Most of all, I acknowledge our re-markable clients who have shared so freely their struggles and triumphs. Thanks to you all for helping to make this book a reality.

Gregg Jantz, Ph.D.

1

People who lose weight permanently are

FREE FROM THE TANGLES OF DIETING

The best way to lose weight is to get the flu
and take a trip to Egypt.
Roz Lawrence

As the cover says, this is *not* a diet book. Not a book on weight loss with low-fat recipes . . . and not another volume swimming in an ocean of *lose fat* books that encourage you to add even more stress to your body through roller coaster weight management programs that only exacerbate the challenges you already face. Instead, the central idea throughout these nine chapters is what we now know to be the only kind of *thinking* that works: it is the whole-person approach. And it is an approach desperately needed, largely because of statistics like the following from the National Institutes of Health and elsewhere:

- It's estimated that one in three Americans is overweight, an increase of thirty percent in the last ten years.

- Forty-four percent of high school girls and fifteen percent of high school boys report that they are trying to lose weight.

13

- Fifty percent of adult females and twenty-four percent of adult males are on a diet on any given occasion.

- It's now estimated that ten percent of Americans have disordered eating.

So, as a nation we have a problem—a serious problem. Unfortunately, the battle of the bulge for most is not getting any easier. That's why we are concerned about people and their weight challenges. But, unlike other weight-loss programs, we do not isolate weight as a single issue. We don't focus on the use of scales or on a daily regimen of checking to see how much has been lost or gained in the last week. Our whole-person approach does not encourage people to tally calories, check body fat, or count cholesterol and sodium. This is because people who lose weight permanently do not rely on the stuff most diets are made of.

"Progress . . . not Perfection"

Instead of working toward perfection in weight management, the two percent who succeed inch toward progress. They come to understand that food is not the issue, because *if food were the problem, then diets would be the answer.* People who lose weight permanently understand they no longer need to rely on food for solace and comfort.

No longer do such people feel trapped and immobilized by weight. Instead, they begin to see themselves as individuals for which the issue of weight is only one component. That is the exhilarating thing about this approach. And that same excitement can be yours as you work through the material in these chapters. While your story will be different, there may be similarities to the challenges faced by Carol, a woman I worked with two years ago. Today, Carol describes her life as one she thought she would never live—as different as day and night. But not long ago, this frustrated, angry, out-of-control mother realized that if she didn't get help there would be no hope for her.

The diet mentality is based on the belief that *thin is good* and *fat is bad*. People begin dieting to become thin and good, only to set in motion an endless cycle of pain and dieting failure.

When I started seeing Carol for weight counseling, she had already been on thirteen different diets, none of which had worked. In fact, after each diet fiasco Carol always

> **Carol's Old Pattern:**
> **Take it off . . . put it on . . .**
> **take it off . . . put more on.**

gained back the weight she lost, plus a few extra pounds. You can imagine how large she'd become after putting her body through such intense shock over so many years. I'd estimated that since junior high Carol had probably shed a total of three to four hundred pounds. Yet she continued to begin every diet with a vague sense of hope that *this one will work . . . I know I'll make it this time. . . . Just one more shot at this and I'll be thin. . . . I know I'll be successful with this one.*

But every diet was just another breathtaking roller coaster ride of self-delusion and false promises, with her depression dipping lower each time as yet one more diet proved painful and ineffective. During and after each unsuccessful diet experience, Carol's highs were high and her lows lower than low. The pain was so great she thought of taking her life on more than one occasion. She had come to the end of the line. She now knew that diets didn't work and never would. Her question was what *would* work?

How did this terrible diet mania start? What put Carol on the hopeless path of eating disorders in the first place? What had gone on in her past to create a foundation of pain that dogged her steps well into adulthood? In our first counseling session, Carol told me her mother had started putting her on diets at the age of thirteen, when she was in sixth grade. At that time, Carol was the largest person in her class. The boys ridiculed her for her size. On more than one occasion she heard her friends laughing behind her back. She would fight back the tears when she heard them calling her "cow" and

> **Carol's Old False Belief: Jelly donuts and ice cream are my faithful friends.**

"pig" and "monster." Deep inside she knew they were right. That *was* how she looked. Worse yet, it was how she felt about herself.

Her weight made her look older than she was. She was a child in an oversized adult's body. Since she had no real friends at school, she began to walk down a path I have seen all too often—a journey that embraced an intimate, negative relationship with food.

Diets, Pills, and Weight-Loss Doctors

Carol would sneak snacks during recess, hide food in her desk, and pilfer sandwiches and cookies from the lunch bags of fellow students. Several times a week on the way home from school, she would pay homage to the corner grocery store where candy, jelly donuts, and half gallons of ice cream were waiting to be her friends. All that food had to go someplace, and without any exercise or care for her body, Carol just got larger and larger.

Her mother assumed the only way for Carol to reduce her weight was to go on a diet, and then another, and then another. After all, the tabloids at the supermarket printed oversized headlines about the overnight diet success of one skinny celebrity after another. The women's magazines she read promised miracles if the overweight person would just eat this, not eat that, take this pill, buy this potion, drink this shake. Whatever was printed about dieting, Carol's mother made sure her daughter tried it, no matter how extreme.

When the diets didn't work—and they never did—she began taking Carol to different doctors in town—weight specialists, they were called—but even ritual appearances in the offices of these medicine men and women did not work. So she began buying diet pills for her daughter, thinking that surely pills would do the trick. They would work for a while, and then Carol would get sick, so her mother would try another brand of false promises.

Fill in the blanks:
1. My problem with food is

_____

2. Besides food, how else do I avoid thinking about hurt in my life? _____

During this ordeal, Carol's mother would put her on a scale three to four times a day, hoping, searching, praying for those two or three illusive pounds that somehow miraculously might have fallen from Carol's body. But the needle on the scale invariably went right instead of left. Carol would stand on the scale and cry as the scale confirmed what she knew would be true: another one, two, three, four, or five pounds. Without knowing it, her mother had set Carol up for failure. She continued to look for the magic pill, the overnight answer, the one diet that would help her daughter shed her unwanted weight, all to no avail. Carol was learning a lot about dieting. She was also learning that her body was not her friend.

The average person coming to The Center for counseling about weight challenges has been on at least seven diets. These men and women have learned to count calories automatically, have an obsession with cholesterol, know as much about packaged diet foods as the manufacturers of those foods, have fasted, eaten only herbs, wracked their bodies with liposuction, and had their stomachs stapled. Desperate people do desperate things. The trouble is that most desperate people do the *wrong things*. People who lose weight permanently dismount the roller coaster of dieting. People who lose weight permanently realize their lives must no longer revolve around food. They know they must take control of their lives and start living as God, their heavenly Father and faithful Friend, intended them to live—with freedom, joy, and an all-abiding sense of self-worth.

Diets—an American Seduction

People who succeed at weight loss recognize the deceit of diets and no longer choose to be victimized by one of the most unregulated industries on record. We now know that women who focus on TV ads about dieting or diet products eat nearly twice as much as those who watch ads about other consumer products. Your first line of defense if you are one of these victims? *Change the channel.* It can be your first step toward taking control of your new life.

Something to think about: Research suggests that women who pay attention to TV ads about dieting eat nearly twice as much as those who focus on ads about other products.

An obsession with dieting has never worked and it never will. Diets hurt you mentally and physically. You lose the weight; you gain it back. You feel good about yourself for a moment, and then you feel terrible. Diets are a cruel joke of bait and switch. You've been conned into thinking you are buying one thing and end up stuck with something else. Have you ever thought of this? *If diets worked, everyone would be thin.* Diets are a kind of Russian roulette. And the game can be deadly. Yet somehow we figure the odds are in our favor so we pay our money and take our chances. After all, like Carol, we think, *Well, maybe this one will work.* We're seduced by full-page, four-color promises, paid celebrity testimonials, newspaper and glamour magazine advertisements, and European "miracle" stories of instant fat removal. There is no end to the deceit. Nor is there a lack of the vulnerable who'll do anything to be thin and therefore be loved, admired, and accepted.

Do I know what dieting is doing to my body? Do I care? If so, am I ready to rethink my problem of weight?

Both the initial and ultimate false premise of a diet is that *food is the culprit.* Food is *not* the problem, and therefore dieting is not the cure. The antidote to dieting—and this will be a theme throughout the book—is to learn to live an authentic, balanced, healthy life as a person who is growing into the individual God created you to be. This is what I want for you. This is what this book is all about. Will it be a challenge? Yes. Will there be obstacles? Without a doubt. Can you do it? You *can* be among the two percent who lose weight permanently.

However, people can't do this in their own strength, and no one can do it overnight. Each person needs the strong yet gentle support and encouragement of others. For success, they also need to follow the action plans at the end of each chapter. More important, I encourage each reader to take to heart what the Apostle Paul writes to the church at Philippi in chapter 4, verse 13: "I can do everything through him who gives me strength." I hope you believe that verse with all your heart, because God *will* give you strength and courage.

Our heavenly Father made us in his own image and that means we were created beautiful whether we see ourselves as attractive or not. When others reject us, God loves us. When we feel bad about ourselves because of our outward appearances, God continues to respect us, care about us, and regard us as his children.

So what are we really talking about here? Is it not the transformation of our inner person? C. S. Lewis once remarked, and I paraphrase, that **no clever assortment of bad eggs makes a good omelet.** You've got to have good resources, good mental *DNA* for healthy personal growth. When we clean up the chaos on the inside, then *and only then* will we be free to address our external challenges.

> Develop a burning desire to become the special person God created you to be. Make the first move. Quit doing what doesn't work.

That's what Carol finally discovered. She learned that while she was seriously overweight, she had an equally large, loving heart. But her caring heart was carrying the burdens of the world. She had chosen to live with the dysfunctionality of her family—the pain, fear, guilt, and anger of her past. It had become part of her flesh. She had paralyzed herself with the toxicity of her life experience.

After a few sessions she told me, "Dr. Jantz, I feel like I'm a sponge, absorbing all the pain I can. But my sponge is so saturated I just cannot absorb any more." That was the breakthrough moment for Carol. When she realized there was no more room to contain the toxins she carried in her body, she realized she needed to do something to quit sabotaging her life. People who lose weight permanently learn to realign their thinking. They choose a life of balance. Their thinking moves from *desperation* about weight to *decisiveness* about losing weight to *a plan* of how to carry out their decision.

Conversely, desperate people play the weight-loss game at random. They are loose canons poised for yet another shipwreck of dieting which only exacerbates further eating disorders.

The ninety-eight percent who will not succeed in losing weight permanently buy all the diet books and weight-loss videos, read—and believe—all the ads and all the fads; join one, two, or even three health clubs; take everyone's advice, professional or not, while all the time they are really doing one thing: standing in line at the roller coaster office saying to the ticket taker,

Take me for a ride again. I know it probably won't be effective, but I'm game. Someday it just may work and who knows . . . *today just may be my lucky day.*

People who lose weight permanently back off from insipid conventional wisdom because they've learned it is nonsense. They quit grazing in the diet aisle of the local book store. They turn the page fast when they come across a diet ad in a magazine. They change the channel immediately when a paid celebrity spokesperson speaks of the miraculous results of the latest, greatest, most fool proof weight-loss program in history. They learn to become more decisive, more selective, more in tune with themselves. They decide to face their worst fears because they know it is the only way they will ever address their deepest pain.

They look their shame, jealousy, rage, anger, and physical, mental, or sexual abuse in the eye and call it what it is. Why do they do this? Because they now know their internal angst

21

has compelled them to think less than kindly of themselves and has forced them to turn to food as their friend.

No Longer in Bondage to Rules

You may be asking, "What is the formula then for success that can put me among the two percent who succeed in losing weight permanently?" The good news is there *is* no formula. There is no set of rules for you to follow. Guidelines and action plans? Yes, but no formulas.

People who lose weight permanently learn that weight loss comes through personal freedom and a *lack of rules*. Rules kill; freedom gives birth to personal growth. Rules immobilize; freedom allows people to be who they are designed to be and gives hope to last a lifetime.

People who are overweight do not have defects in their personalities. Instead, they choose to live with pain *and food has been a way to cope with that pain*. That's what Carol finally discovered. She realized there were many unkind people in her life who judged her cruelly—starting with her classmates in junior high. Later it was uncaring neighbors, relatives, and acquaintances who judged her harshly when she became an adult.

These critics jumped to the conclusion that because she was overweight there was something wrong with her. *Carol no longer believes that.* She has forgiven those who abused her in the past, and she is learning to offer forgiveness to those who attempt to hurt her in the present. She has now become an honored member of that two percent group for whom food is no longer the issue, and it all started when she made the conscious decision to deal with *real issues*.

In our counseling sessions we never focused on Carol's weight. In fact, we seldom talked about it. We did, however, address the emotional poisons she had chosen to live with for so long and offered her a way of healthy escape. Now, just as Carol received help, I urge you to look inside your own life and past experiences.

What emotional toxins are you living with? What pain, fear, hurt, frustration, or abuse have become so much a part of your inner world that you have difficulty differentiating it from life itself? If you have chosen food as your weapon against these toxins, you are probably aware that the

> You have an exciting, new assignment: learning how to love yourself again. All this time you've been searching for two elusive things: love and acceptance. Now they are both within reach, because you are finally providing them for yourself, based on God's love for you.

battle will never be won. You will struggle on in vain. In fact, your present life may seem more like you are pouring gasoline on a fire and hoping the fuel will put out the flame.

A Definition of Insanity

One popular definition of insanity is **doing the same thing over and over and expecting a different result.** You need to know that food is not the cure for your pain. If you choose not to believe this, the tangle, deceit, and empty promises of diets will only further confuse and exacerbate the challenges you face. The key to your better, more hopeful future is to deal with your pain and address your *real* problems.

"But you don't know my mother . . . or father . . . or brother . . . or aunt. It's not easy being around them. They're always judging me because of my weight, telling me about the latest diet and making me feel bad about myself."

No, but Carol does. Carol's mother, now eighty-seven years old, remains obsessed with food and dieting as she continues to live in her own vast, isolated wasteland of judgment and denial. She has become a master of knowing how to take that prickly thorn of judgment and wiggle it deep into her daughter's side. "You're still not good enough, Carol. Come on, here's another diet for you. You're starting to gain again, little one. Isn't it time we see another doctor about your weight?" This is hard for Carol to hear, but she now knows it's simply not true. That's why she's made a daily commitment to forgive her mother. Her mother's abusive comments sting but no longer destroy. They no longer hurt as they once did because Carol has dealt with the real issues in her life, and participating in the false promises of her mother and the deceit of a 30-billion-dollar weight-loss industry are no longer among them.

Carol has learned that a lean body is not the answer to the stresses of life. Not even the recent discovery of a hormone called *leptin* that makes mice skinny—and holds great promise for humans—is throwing Carol off track. No longer does Carol pay inordinate attention to every morsel of food she eats. She does not exercise compulsively.

She has learned that the weight and shape of her body are not the determining factors of who she is and what she is becoming. Diets taught Carol—and teach us all—to regard food as the source of our weight challenges. But since we now know this is a blatant falsehood, the only result from believing this lie will be more obsessive activity, further frustration, and even more self-sabotaging behavior.

Diets chip away at an already fragile self-esteem, taking the dieter up and then down yet another roller coaster of false hope and empty promises. Like the ancient Egyptian sphinx or the Parthenon on the Acropolis in Athens that suffer the ravages of weather and an increasingly polluted environment, diets have their insidious way of eating away at the best of who you are—and you may not even know it is happening.

Covenant with Myself
The 30-billion-dollar weight-loss industry no longer will receive my financial or emotional support. With my signature below, I covenant never to purchase their products or believe their empty promises again.

Signed _____

The good news is that you can reverse the trend. There is hope that you can and will be among that select two percent who will succeed in losing weight permanently because you now know it's really an *inside job*. Beginning now, you can choose to refuse to be a victim of the aggressive marketing of diet programs put into place by those who never have and never will care whether you lose weight permanently.

Starting today, you no longer need accept the shame heaped on you by family members who've always had "your best interest" in mind. Starting right now, I want you to take as your life's motto, "progress, not perfection."

Health, Balance, and Forgiveness

What about Carol today? It's been one year since I've spoken with her. She told me that since she had completed counseling she's had only one regression. One week her stress level was so high that she binged for three days.

The difference this time was that *she knew what she was doing* and was able to correct herself. She knew she was acting out the pain of her past, but was quickly able to say, This behavior does not define who I am or what I am becoming, nor is it how I want to live my life. With God's help and her own determined effort, she realigned herself with her core beliefs: health, balance, personal growth, forgiveness, and feeling good about herself. This is the hallmark of those who lose weight permanently.

As Alcoholics Anonymous reminds us, it is **"progress, not perfection"** that provides the ingredient for success. That's what Carol has learned, and as you look inside yourself, it will also be one of the keys to your own personal growth. Carol no longer diets and no longer weighs herself. They are both unnecessary. She now laughingly asks, What does weight have to do with anything? She has learned to face her fears—those false poisons that made her emotionally sick for so long.

Carol learned to jump off the high dive and started believing in herself. The more she took courageous leaps, the easier it became the next time. Carol is not the same person who walked into my office two years ago. She is now confident, caring, forgiving, and loving beyond measure. When she quit focusing on her weight, when she threw away the diet books, when she realized her outer appearance bore no resemblance to the great-hearted person she was inside, then Carol joined the ranks of those who were on track to lose weight permanently.

I hope you catch the excitement as we come to the end of this chapter, because soon we will have the joy of saying the same thing about you. It's our prayer that this book will be the first step of a magnificent journey that will take you where you want to go.

The more high dives you take, and the more willing you are to accept assistance from those who care deeply about you, the faster you will rebuild the self-confidence and self-esteem that God has already given you. *There is nothing wrong with you.* You are not defective. You just need to change the oil, tune the engine, and get back in the driver's seat.

You've weathered some great turbulence with diets that haven't worked. You've perhaps exhibited some extreme behavior for which you are not proud. Lightning has struck close by and you've had some close calls. You may have had your stomach stapled, mouth wired, dieted yourself almost to death, and had everything tucked that could be tucked. But that is all in the past. None of that matters now because you are on an exciting new pilgrimage of courage and hope.

God has preserved you for a reason: to grow you into the loving, caring person he designed you to be. Your body has proven to be resilient. This means you can go back and recapture the health and vitality you once enjoyed.

You *can* lose weight permanently and be among the two percent who succeed, and this great venture can start today by paying careful attention to the Action Plans and begin working them. They appear at the end of each chapter. If you have any current health concerns, be sure to check with your medical doctor before making changes.

Action Plan #1

Say Good-bye to Your Crutches

1. You no longer need to weigh yourself *because weight is no longer the issue.* Ask yourself: Do I want to weigh a certain amount, or do I want to feel good about myself and my life? Here's what I want you to do. Put your bathroom scale in a closet or in the attic where you can get to it if necessary. But try to avoid using it. It's a crutch.

2. If you have unopened, packaged *diet food* that's been in your cupboard for months, wrap it up and put it in the box with the items that follow in #3. You don't need this food anymore. *It's a crutch.*

3. You may have items of clothing you've been hanging on to since you fit into a size four or five: a pair of jeans you wore in high school, or a bathing suit that looked terrific when you were twenty-one. You may have worn those clothes to draw attention to your body when you were starving yourself down to 101 pounds. Now, you continue to hang on to the false belief that you'll once again get into them. (You might, but not for the same reasons.) Put all those items of clothing in a box with the packaged food and secure it with strapping tape strong enough to make it difficult to open.

4. Now place the sealed box in your attic or storeroom, where you know you can get to it if necessary. Then, in big black letters write on the box: FALSE CRUTCHES. Put today's date on the box. You no longer need those tangibles to help you lose weight. However, if you ever feel you need to wear or eat what's in the box, go get it. We're not taking things away from you. We are only creating distance between you and the things which are guaranteed to impede your progress.

People who lose weight permanently take the initiative and remove all false crutches from their lives and begin living from the inside out. I know this is your desire or you would not be reading this book. Please carry out each of the suggestions in this Action Plan now, because they have been clinically proven to help protect you from sneak attacks which are sure to come—the theme of chapter 2.

2

People who lose weight permanently want

NO MORE SNEAK ATTACKS

I've been on a diet for two weeks, and all I've lost is two weeks.

Totie Fields

One bright, sunny day a young farm boy ran up to his grand-dad who was returning from the field. "Grandpa, quick, tell me, how much time do I have?" Granddad answered, "You have just enough time, son."

"But how much time will it take for me to be big and grown up like you?" the boy asked, tugging on his grandpa's pant leg. The old man smiled. "Just like everything else, my boy, it will take just the right amount of time."

"Why do I have to be a boy? Why do I have to wait so long? Why can't I just be a man—like you?" the boy asked, frustration now filling his young face. Grandpa kneeled down and looked his grandson straight in the eye, saying, "Son, when you do one thing right—at the right time—the next thing works even better and you one day will become what you want to become."

Time Is a Friend

Time! It's our most precious asset. To think otherwise can lead us to overwhelming regret, frustration, and even despair. Even though we may not speak of it much in this book, these pages are actually all about time—about the critical 24 hours a day and 168 hours a week we have to choose our direction in life. We all wish we had more time to accelerate our spiritual and emotional growth, but that is physically impossible. No one can give us that gift of extra time. But we don't need any more time to join the two percent who permanently lose weight. We have all the time we need.

Time is not the issue. Too little time will never keep us from achieving our goals and objectives. The challenge is the decision and the dedication to move in the direction of our dreams. Doing it right the first time will always require less time. There is a time for everything, and each time is a preparation for the next. We have just enough time for everything we need to do. The rest is busywork. Nothing that is important to our personal growth can be hurried up. We are growing oaks, not sunflowers. One takes years, the other a few dog days of summer, but long after the seasons have sent the sunflower packing, the oak continues to put its roots deeper and deeper.

> In the challenge to reach a goal, there is only one way to move: forward.

The Paradigm Shift

The word *paradigm* is important because it is a model, a standard, a principle or assumption which we all tend to accept as if we were flying on automatic pilot. We would be lost without paradigms in our lives because they help us stay on course. However, there comes a time when we must look at what makes us tick and ask questions about what we've been thinking that has not been working in our lives. That's when a paradigm shift is essential to our growth, possibly even to our survival. The following story says it best.

Two battleships assigned to the training squadron had been at sea on maneuvers in heavy weather for several days. The visibility was poor with patchy fog, so the captain remained on the bridge keeping an eye on all activities.

Shortly after dark, the lookout on the wing of the bridge reported, "Light, bearing on the starboard bow."

"Is it steady or moving astern?" the captain called out.

The lookout replied, "Steady, captain," which meant they were on a dangerous collision course with that ship.

The captain then called to the signalman, "Signal that ship: We are on a collision course; advise you change course 20 degrees."

Back came a signal, "Advise that YOU change course 20 degrees."

The captain said, "Send this message: I'm a captain; change course 20 degrees."

"I'm a seaman second class," came the reply. "You had better change course 20 degrees."

By that time, the captain was furious. He spat out, "Send: I am a battleship. Change course 20 degrees."

Back came the flashing light, "I am a lighthouse."

The ship changed course.

People who lose weight permanently know they must engage in a similar paradigm shift if they are to be counted among the two percent. Remember our practical definition of insanity? Doing the same thing again and again, while always expecting—and hoping for—a different result. If your results are always the same and you don't like what you see, a paradigm shift is in order.

People who rely on diets, advertising hype, binges, purges, and pills to lose weight are living with the same ineffective paradigm. Perhaps this is you. You've been swimming in the same waters of weight loss for years, struggling to swim upstream, fighting the current, and worrying whether you were going to keep your weary head above water. Even though you had the best of intentions, you never quite made it. So you took a breather, read some of the latest diet books, bought some expensive exercise equipment promoted by a celebrity on a late-night television infomercial, believed the tabloid headlines, and said, *Yes, now I've got it. Finally I have the answer.* So you jumped back into the water and started paddling against the same current, fighting the familiar, unforgiving current all the way saying, *Yes, yes, I can do it; I know I'll make it this time . . .* only to succumb to a numbing fatigue which discouraged you, frightened you, and set you up for yet another bout with failure.

> **Those who carry out the Action Plans at the end of each chapter will be one step further on the way to permanent weight loss.**

If this sounds like you, then you have chosen the right book. In these pages we won't talk about diets or any other forms of extreme weight-management techniques. People who permanently lose weight don't need to be extreme. People who lose weight permanently learn to jump into the same water but this time the current does not sweep them away. There is no swimming upstream, fearing that drowning is imminent. People who lose weight permanently work with the current. They do not resist it. Diets and programs of self-deprivation teach people to set up a resistance to growth which is the opposite result they are seeking. The unfortunate truth is that *dieting often establishes a pattern of eating disorders that persists for a lifetime*. We're death on diets because diets are death on you.

That's the purpose of this chapter—to help readers keep from sabotaging the successes they are already beginning to enjoy as they join the ranks of the two percent. Make the decision to believe that diets don't work. That's the first important step. Now what? If diets don't work, what does? Well, first of all, you do. You work, and always have. If you don't agree, you simply have not shifted the paradigm of weight loss possibilities far enough to realize that you already own the answers to the challenges of being overweight. Now is the time to close the chapter on an ineffective past and open a new chapter that will lead to your better, brighter future.

Those who have achieved permanent weight loss have found that diets set them on a course for other problems unrelated to food. In fact, they may have gone completely out of control and found themselves in an emotional tailspin, even using more dieting as a means of control. When they could find no reliable friend, they turned to food as a companion. But they discovered the very thing they tried to use as a solution to their problems exacerbated them, bringing even more emotional and physical pain.

It's a fact: *diet fads last about a year.* But weight management lasts a lifetime. Diets come and go. But successful people don't. Clinical tests demonstrate that people who lose weight permanently are victorious because they refuse to rely on external techniques and gimmicks for their personal growth.

You Are Not a Sickness

You may have been victimized by the medical model which says: If you keep sabotaging yourself and can't lose weight on your own, then you must have a disease. Your obesity is a disease. Your eating is a disease, so we'd better give you some pills or suggest surgery. How about some staples in your stomach? That hopefully will do the trick. After all, it's not your fault you have this disease, but we assure you that some medication or invasive treatment will cure it.

> **Emotional challenges + obsessive behavior = excessive weight.**

You are not a disease. Do not allow any well-intentioned, medically trained person to persuade you that you are. You are a person with emotional challenges that have taken the form of obsessive-compulsive behavior that has translated into excessive weight. That is where you must start, because from this honest premise you can move into a personal, self-corrective program where you can join the two percent who lose weight permanently.

We're not going to talk about steps—twelve, fifteen, twenty, or one hundred. For weight loss, there is but one step in the right direction. People who lose weight permanently do not attend groups that treat them like victims, where they sit in a circle and talk about their powerlessness. What a disservice to say that we have no power! Of course we have power, and plenty of it. (The Twelve Steps of Alcoholics Anonymous make it clear—we have power through our Higher Power.) That's why it's vital to treat the whole person, not just a single part. Why does this work? Because rather than wallowing in a mire of powerlessness, people can learn to regain and reassert their power. They start to engage in a healthy self-focus, not narcissism. To become intimately acquainted with their deepest troubles and hurts means attaining a self-knowledge that allows them to look at their own souls with tender compassion, something they may not have done for some time. In the process, they learn that power has been given to them by their heavenly Father.

You may have been told it was your upbringing that made you overweight. It's not your family, nor is it how your uncle, aunt, or grandmother raised you. You may think, *I can't help it. We lived on a farm and all we ate was meat, potatoes, and apple pie à la mode.* Of course your early environment plays a role in every area of your life. But now you are an adult and adolescent excuses are no longer in order.

> **You become empowered when you provide yourself with four things:**
> - **Discipline**
> - **Freedom**
> - **Acceptance of the truth that you are deeply loved**
> - **Courage to face your fears**

People who lose weight permanently move beyond blaming others for their weight. They take responsibility for their own actions because they know it's the only way they will ever grow into the person God created them to be. People who lose weight permanently also learn to take full responsibility for their own emotional state of being. Blaming family is the easy way out, and it's a dead-end street. Perhaps the theme song of those who lose weight permanently should be the great spiritual that reminds us, "Not my sister, not my brother, but it's me, O Lord, standing in the need of prayer." Yes, Lord it's me . . . and it's you.

> **Encouragement from God's Word:** Therefore, my dear brothers [and sisters], stand firm. Let nothing move you. Always give yourselves fully to the work of the Lord, because you know that your labor in the Lord is not in vain.
> 1 Corinthians 15:58

Never again do you need to be controlled by external forces. Nor do you need to control everything as you used to when you paddled upstream, muscling your way through the current by using ineffective weight-loss programs. Whatever you choose to control will ultimately control you. You don't need to be controlled by anything other than the Holy Spirit who has been assigned to you as a Comforter and Friend for all the areas of your life—including your weight. Now just how practical can God get?

Here is something else to help move you even closer to your goal of permanent weight loss:

Affirmations to Help You Re-nurture Yourself

- I like who I am and what I am becoming. I know I have been created in God's image and that God only creates what is precious.

- I know that my weight has nothing to do with my ability to love others and reach out to those in need.

- I am a person who no longer judges myself or my many abilities based on my weight.

- I now feel joy, not shame, about myself—even as my body is in transition. I am not where I want to be, but thank God, I'm also not where I once was.

- I am now taking control of my weight challenge and no longer see myself as controlled by my family's past or other external circumstances.

- I demonstrate self-respect at all times, even as I show respect for all those I meet—regardless of their weight, gender, or personality type.

- I am learning to relax as I prepare to join the two percent who lose weight permanently.

- I am daily moving closer to my goal of permanent weight loss. I am not getting frustrated if progress is slow, as I am interested in progress, not perfection.

- I know and believe with all my being that I can do all things through Christ, who gives me strength.

- We ask people who come to The Center to put affirmations like these on 3x5 cards and repeat them aloud several times a day. You, too, will discover the power of these thoughts as you make them yours and as you honestly come to believe them. You *are* what you say and think about all day long. That's why affirmations such as these can help you achieve your goal of permanent weight loss.

Forget the Image

In Charles Colson's thoughtful editorial "The Superwaif: Pandering to Perversity" he writes:

"Feed me," said the graffiti sprawled across an outdoor advertisement. "Give me a cheeseburger," said another slogan. Beneath the spray paint you can see a super-skinny model, lying face down on a couch and wearing Calvin Klein's newest perfume—and nothing else.

It's Kate Moss, and she embodies what's called the "waif" look: very young and thin. Some women's groups are protesting that the look promotes anorexia—that it sells a message of starvation along with high fashion.

But, of course, it also sells something much more serious: the image of adolescent girls as sexual objects. . . .

In some ads, the suggestion of sexual prey is even more explicit. In one photo, Kate Moss cringes nude in the corner of a sofa, her arms pressed across her chest as though warding off an assault. She's also been photographed with her eyes bruised, looking distressed with her hand over her mouth. . . .

What's worse, these photos are not concealed in plain paper wrappings. They're found in glossy fashion magazines on store shelves; they're plastered on the sides of buses and bus stops—where all of us are forced to see them as we walk city streets.

Exploitation of this sort ought to bring out the holy rage in every one of us. The most important mark of a civilization is how it treats its most vulnerable members. Ads that suggest sexual violence against children are a sure sign that the barbarians are in our midst.

While the above editorial demonstrates the tragedy of the waif image, *Newsweek* (11 September 1995) reports on the zanier side of the pandering—a questionable "beauty tip" from Japan called "navel nirvana":

> Summer sends women in search of the perfect bathing suit, the perfect tan, the perfect . . . belly button? In Japan, mid-baring fashions . . . have inspired some women to turn to plastic surgery for navel nirvana. For those willing to hand over $1,000, a 20-minute procedure can transform a normal round hole into a "prettier" vertical slit. Tokyo's Jujin Hospital alone has stitched almost 100 buttons this year; more requests are rolling in.

I quote the above because this constant barrage of images has the power to sabotage the progress of those who are on their way to permanent weight loss. That's why we must all change the channel or turn the other way when we see or hear a diet ad, a paper-thin celebrity touting some exercise fad, or any other form of sexually exploitive advertisement. These attempt to seduce us into accepting a quick fix, no sweat, no problem, you'll-lose-a-pound-an-hour hoax. These sneak attacks can sabotage our objective of permanent weight loss. It's up to us to refuse to buy into them.

Family Food Patterns

Before we pin the whole rap on the media, let's look at some of the areas in our own lives where these self-sabotaging behaviors may have begun. First, some questions about your parents may provide insight into your present situation:

- Did your father refer to adult women as *women* or *girls?*

- Did he show you respect?

- Was it a "macho" household where your father ruled with an iron fist or a strongly led home where individuals were appreciated?

- How were the women in your home treated?

- If you are a man and as a child weren't aggressive, did members of your family ever imply that you might be gay, weak, wimpy, or just a boy—regardless of your age?

- Were women considered a powerful or powerless force in your family?

- Did your parents share the workload—such as meals, laundry, yard work, child-care?

- What were the male/female background patterns that taught you to be unhappy with yourself and therefore pushed you toward food as your primary source of comfort?

- Were men in your family viewed as the ones in control whereas women were there to serve?

The questions could go on indefinitely, but here's what I'm getting at. If you grew up in a home where the men (father, stepfather, brothers, uncles) had all the answers, then you were raised in an environment where there was great risk for weight gain as a way of coping with your stress, even though the anxiety may have been unconscious. What were your other choices? Not many. You didn't throw bricks through windows; you didn't quit bathing or engage in other socially unacceptable behaviors, but you did begin to gain weight. You probably said, "Hey, everyone has to eat, and it sure feels good to me. In fact, food feels like a great friend." So you ate, and ate, and ate, and ate.

Eating as self-help is little more than an alternative "medicine" for something we either do not understand or do not know exists. But it only further aggravates the symptoms and makes the patient sicker, more despondent, often to the point of despair. Earlier I spoke of not blaming our families for our problems of weight, but rather accepting our home environments as facts of our early lives. Research tells us that our food patterns are set around the age of five. But like anything else, we can change those patterns as adults and start enjoying the exciting journey of becoming the persons we desire to be. Therefore, if you can gain a clearer perspective on what happened in your youthful past, you will be in a better position. Awareness is the first step toward better emotional health and a brighter future.

Sneak Attack at Church

As we begin to understand our past, we also learn to understand the present. And that will help us identify "sneak attacks" when they come. Even at church. Really. For some people sneak attacks have occurred (or may continue to occur) in the friendly fellowship environment of the church. Church is a God-honoring place for fellowship, so why not enjoy it all—including the extra fellowship around the table loaded with chocolate donuts, devil's food cake, apple pies, fried chicken dinners with mashed potatoes and gravy, salads heaped with mayonnaise, all topped off with more ice cream than a fellowship-hungry person ought to have!

I have counseled many clients over the years who've told me that this scenario was their life. Music and meringue, faith and fellowship, piety and pie! But before long, the fellowship of the overcomers becomes the fellowship of the overeaters. These clients—and, perhaps you—always saw it as the social thing to do.

Then one day someone at church, probably a male, said, "Sister, you're putting on a few pounds, aren't you?" He may even have been blunt enough to say, "You know, I hate to say it but you're getting fat!" Ouch! That hurt. It also confused you. You were doing what you thought was right: eating socially at church. Your alleged sin was now out in the open, and you felt you were in good company. But the unkind comment started to make you feel shame. Strangely, instead of moving away from food, you actually edged closer to it. The sneak attack not only worked, but you fell for it hook, line, and sinker. In fact, that pattern may still be hurting you today.

An overeater may be digging a grave with his or her teeth.

This could have happened anywhere: in your church, at a social service club where you felt obligated to eat, perhaps at school, or in your home where you heard people say, "Honey, clean your plate. Don't you know there are millions of children in China who are starving and would just love to have that potato skin or thin piece of lettuce or last morsel of meat on that chicken leg?" Another sneak attack. And you may have taken the guilt to heart, which is only a short distance to your stomach. Is it possible that you have never left a plate with food on it since? Still, you've always wanted to be thin—like the people on television, in the movies, in the diet ads, or in the gym.

Models: Thin-waisted Sneak Attacks

Here's an exercise I encourage you to complete right now—while you are reading this page. This is for your eyes only, so please be honest with your response.

Five People Who Are My Physical Role Models

1. _____
2. _____
3. _____
4. _____
5. _____

What people did you put on your list? Who are your past and present role models based on their physical appearance? Calcutta's beloved Mother Teresa? Israel's former Prime Minister Golda Meir? I don't think so. But if I suggested that they might be people such as Cindy Crawford, Richard Gere, Madonna, Tom Cruise, Janet Jackson, Courtney Love, the tanned, toned, and thin stars on *General Hospital* or *Days of Our Lives*, or any number of other men and women on the Hollywood scene, I'd probably be getting closer to the kind of person you would most like to look like.

There are two challenges here:

1. Part of the self-sabotaging behavior for these celebrities themselves is sex-related. They know they are people created in the image of Madison Avenue, Hollywood, the talent agencies, and the media spin doctors. They know they are more "properties" than people. With a few notable exceptions, they have bought the concept that their bodies have one objective: to sell a product.

2. These role models can pull you away from your goal. You don't need models to tell you how you need to look. How you feel about yourself must not depend on how tiny your waist is, the size of your breasts, whether you've starved yourself into a size three, and whether you've had your face, buttocks, or thighs tucked and retucked.

Three things I have learned so far that help me understand how I can join the two percent:

1. _____
2. _____
3. _____

People who lose weight permanently know they may, in fact, become slender again—but for an entirely different reason. They see weight loss as a byproduct of becoming a constantly growing, more emotionally healthy person. The good news is that we've come a long way from the painful days of such practices as struggling into corsets and binding feet.

Corsets and Footbinding

Every civilization attempts to shape the outward look of its citizens. In the days when girdles and corsets were prominent, as much as eighty pounds of pressure was applied to women's abdomens for one reason alone: to make them appear thinner and more beautiful. In China, footbinding was a traditional custom where the feet of young girls were tightly bound with strips of linen to prevent further growth. The large toe was bent backward over the top of the foot, and the remaining toes were folded underneath. Girls between the ages of five and twelve were selected to undergo this torture, especially if they gave promise of future beauty. Once begun, the process could not be reversed. The pain was excruciating as this deformity remained with the women for the rest of their lives. Starting as a symbol of beauty, it later came to be a requirement for a bride. To its credit, in 1912 the Chinese government officially banned the custom.

You and I may cringe at the emotional and physical torment inflicted on innocent Chinese women for so many years. But around us we see "mindbinding" that similarly creates a distorted and unnatural idea of beauty. Uncaring, unconcerned marketers use sex and slenderness as their ploy to sell widgets.

Diets: Blatant Sneak Attacks

We've mentioned the beauty industry. The diet industry also sells us a bill of goods. Let's summarize:

- Diets promote competition and comparison. They make us objects—not people.

- Through diets we give our power to others. Our emotions are dictated by what registers on the bathroom scale. Our day can be destroyed in an instant if we wake up, weigh ourselves, and discover we've gained a pound. That's why we say: Put the scale in the closet!

- We tend to judge ourselves as good or bad depending on whether we are on a diet. Diets create artificial control. They insult our intelligence. Diets impose a moral judgment, and they distort reality.

45

■ Diets teach and perpetuate mind games. They counsel us to procrastinate: I'll start later, after this big piece of apple pie with ice cream.

■ Diets keep us from success. They block our progress. Friday night you go out for a lovely dinner. But you started your diet the preceding Monday. Now it's dessert time, and you say to yourself, "This has been such a great dinner. I deserve this high-calorie piece of cheese-cake." Bingo! The mind game at work. You eat the dessert and you feel *guilty*. Now you feel so bad about your minor defeat that you go home and clean out the half-gallon of ice cream that's in the fridge. Here's the point. The dessert at the fine restaurant would not have killed you if you had a whole-person approach to weight which does not demand dieting.

My Daughter the Athlete, Please!

I'll call her Sarah. Her father hoped against hope that she would become a famous athlete. There was only one problem. Sarah didn't want to become an athlete. In fact, she wasn't that well coordinated, didn't have much speed on the track, and got more enjoyment just being a spectator at her school's athletic events. But that didn't stop her father. He made Sarah join the softball, volleyball, and basketball teams. On weekends he would take his daughter to the local park and they'd kick soccer balls, hit softballs, run laps, take tennis lessons— all to the point of obsession. There was seldom a night when Sarah did not go to bed in tears. She'd cry out inside, *Dad, I don't want to become an athlete. I hate it. I can't stand it. Why are you making me do all these things I don't want to do?*

Before long, Sarah gravitated to food as her only source of comfort. The love she could not get from her father was available in the refrigerator, in high-fat candy bars, in half gallons of ice cream, and at the local bakery where she became a regular patron each day after school. Before long, Kim ballooned in weight—so large that she could not go to the park anymore with her father. Every movement took her breath away. She could hardly walk, much less run. Finally, she had found a legitimate excuse for not performing on the field. Sarah found a way to put distance between herself and her father's expectations.

> **Carpe diem.**
> **Seize the day.**
> **Decide that today is the day you will seek progress, not perfection, in your program of permanent weight loss.**

Even though the agony of overweight was painful, it provided Sarah relief from the relentless expectations of her father. Obsession with food became her substitute for her father's affection and became the neutral, nondemanding love object she craved. Unfortunately, her father never dealt with his own pathology and continued to berate his daughter for not becoming the person she should have become (read: not becoming the person *he envisioned* his daughter to be). The happy part of this story is that many

> **Forgiveness of those who did you harm in the past is usually your first step toward personal growth, emotional maturity, and permanent weight loss.**

years later Sarah got help. She has now become a proud member of the two percent club—those determined, emotionally healthy souls who lose weight permanently. She recognizes she may never have the privilege of enjoying the father-love she'd always craved, but she also knows that what she missed is no longer a viable adult excuse for remaining overweight. Sarah has forgiven her father and she is getting on with her life.

It has not been easy for Sarah, nor will it necessarily be easy for you. You will never completely arrive. Life will always be filled with challenges, some so great you'll wonder if you'll ever meet them. So with that awareness, I encourage you to step out and face your fears.

Action Plan #2

Say Good-bye to Self-sabotaging Behavior

1. On a separate piece of paper, draw your kitchen table and mark the places where you and the other members of your family sat when you were a child. Go back in time and recreate some of your earliest conversations with your parents, brothers, and sisters. What was said? Who said it? Were you the oldest, youngest? What was mealtime like for you as a youngster?

2. Go through some current or past issues of *Vogue, Cosmopolitan, Redbook, Muscle and Fitness,* or other "beautiful body" magazines and tear out every page that reinforces a negative role about sexuality—one that suggests you need to be glamorous, thin, pumped, or well-endowed to feel good about yourself. Place these pages in a stack and tie them up. Then take them outside where it's safe and legal—to the seashore or to a barbecue pit—and burn them. Watch the false messages go up in smoke, along with the negative programming

that up until now created your self-sabotaging behavior. Then, whenever you feel you are being lured into the glamour trap, remember that the symbols of that deceit have already been consumed by fire and are no longer a threat to you.

3. Complete the blanks:
   As I engage in my commitment to losing weight permanently, I know I first need to have a deeper love and appreciation for myself—the person God created so uniquely. With that goal in mind:

   For me to truly love and appreciate who I am, I need
   _____.

   For me to believe in my heart that I am worthy of being loved, whether I'm thin or not, I must
   _____.

   For me to become more open and loving to others, I need to _____.

4. Write a one-page letter to all the glamorous magazine and television people who up until now have been inappropriate role models for you. Refer to each person by name. Say what you feel about them in your letter. Be free and fully expressive with your words. Tell them how you see them using their sexuality to promote weight-loss programs that are ineffective and deceiving. Then take the letter—along with the magazine pictures in step two—and burn them. Declare that you will never again be persuaded by their lies.

Letting go is what this chapter has been all about. It's letting go of the entrapments that have kept one foot nailed to the floor, forcing you to wander in a vicious circle that's been driving you to distraction and despair. But now you are making progress. Because of what you are learning, you are ready to take a fresh, new look at food. You are now ready to make eating food an art. This is the subject we will address as courageously as possible in chapter 3.

3

People who lose weight permanently learn to view

EATING AS AN ART

Eat a third, drink a third, and then leave the remaining third of your stomach empty. Then, if anger overtakes you, there will be room in it for gas.
The Talmud

In one of the best books written on the difficult subject of forgiveness, *Forgive and Forget,* author Lewis B. Smedes tells a poignant tale that is for all time and for all people. The story hammers home the message that forgiveness is everything or it is nothing. Without it, your life and mine will remain a series of crushing, blaming experiences which will keep us from becoming the people we really want to be.

The tale begins in the village of Faken in innermost Friesland where there lived a long thin baker named Fouke, a righteous man, with a long thin chin and a long thin nose. Fouke was so upright that he seemed to spray righteousness from his thin lips over everyone who came near him; so the people of Faken preferred to stay away.

Fouke's wife, Hilda, was short and round, her arms were round, her bosom was round, her rump was round. Hilda did not keep people at bay with righteousness; her soft

51

roundness seemed to invite them instead to come close to her in order to share the warm cheer of her open heart.

Hilda respected her righteous husband and loved him, too, as much as he allowed her; but her heart ached for something more from him than his worthy righteousness. And there, in the bed of her need, lay the seed of sadness.

One morning, having worked since dawn to knead his dough for the ovens, Fouke came home and found a stranger in his bedroom lying on Hilda's round bosom.

Hilda's adultery soon became the talk of the tavern and the scandal of the Faken congregation. Everyone assumed that Fouke would cast Hilda out of his house, so righteous was he. But he surprised everyone by keeping Hilda as his wife, saying he forgave her as the Good Book said he should.

In his heart of hearts, however, Fouke could not forgive Hilda for bringing shame to his name. Whenever he thought about her, his feelings toward her were angry and hard; he despised her as if she were a common whore. When it came right down to it, he hated her for betraying him after he had been so good and so faithful a husband to her.

He only pretended to forgive Hilda so that he could punish her with his righteous mercy. But Fouke's fakery did not sit well in heaven.

Forgiveness = seeing with new eyes.

So each time that Fouke would feel his secret hate toward Hilda, an angel came to him and dropped a small pebble, hardly the size of a shirt button, into Fouke's heart. Each time a pebble dropped, Fouke would feel a stab of pain like the pain he felt the moment he came on Hilda feeding her hungry heart from a stranger's larder.

Thus he hated her the more; his hate brought him pain and his pain made him hate. The pebbles multiplied. And Fouke's heart grew very heavy with the weight of them, so heavy that the top half of his body bent forward so far that he had to strain his neck upward in order to see straight ahead. Weary with hurt, Fouke began to wish he were dead.

The angel who dropped the pebbles into his heart came to Fouke one night and told him how he could be healed of his hurt. There was one remedy, he said, only one, for the hurt of a wounded heart. Fouke would need the miracle of the magic eyes. He would need eyes that could look back to the beginning of his hurt and see his Hilda, not as a wife who betrayed him, but as a weak woman who needed him. Only a new way of looking at things through the magic eyes could heal the hurt flowing from the wounds of yesterday.

Fouke protested. "Nothing can change the past," he said. "Hilda is guilty, a fact that not even an angel can change."

"Yes, poor hurting man, you are right," the angel said. "You cannot change the past, you can only heal the hurt that comes to you from the past. And you can heal it only with the vision of the magic eyes."

"And how can I get your magic eyes?" pouted Fouke.

"Only ask, desiring as you ask, and they will be given you. And each time you see Hilda through your new eyes, one pebble will be lifted from your aching heart."

Fouke could not ask at once, for he had grown to love his hatred. But the pain of his heart finally drove him to want and to ask for the magic eyes that the angel had promised. So he asked. And the angel gave.

Soon Hilda began to change in front of Fouke's eyes, wonderfully and mysteriously. He began to see her as a needy woman who loved him instead of a wicked woman who betrayed him.

The angel kept his promise; he lifted the pebbles from Fouke's heart, one by one, though it took a long time to take them all away. Fouke gradually felt his heart grow lighter; he began to walk straight again, and somehow his nose and his chin seemed less thin and sharp than before. He invited Hilda to come into his heart again, and she came, and together they began again a journey into their second season of humble joy.[1]

Forgiveness: the great pebble remover, the foremost act that prompts us to get on with our lives in a manner that brings pleasure to us and gives openhearted love to the ones who need forgiveness. Right now, like Fouke's, your heart can become lighter, and you can begin to walk straight again. It's what is destined to happen in your life as you lower the barriers of anger and resentment and let that one important person back in your heart again. It may not be easy, but it is important.

Peter the Victim

Without engaging in this difficult act of forgiveness, no one— including Peter Johnson (not his real name)—would be among the two percent who are in the process of losing weight permanently. In his words, "I had much to learn about myself and about life. I'd been blaming others for years for my problem with weight. I came to understand that to intentionally forgive those who hurt me would give me the permission to put my life back together. I didn't understand it at first, but I needed to forgive my parents in order to move toward a life of permanent weight loss. This meant I also needed a new view of what food was and what it had become to me. Finally, after so much pain, blaming and regret, I'm beginning to learn how to look at eating as an art."

Peter is forty-four years old. He grew up in a politically and religiously conservative family. An outside observer would probably say that his was an emotionally healthy family. They went to church, were good citizens, paid their taxes, and were treated with respect in the community. They had it made. However, there was more to the story, as there always is. Peter grew up in a family with three older brothers. From day one Peter was treated as the baby, the last born, the one who needed to be perpetually nurtured. His mother smothered him with inappropriate caregiving as she became involved in every detail of his life. Peter was never allowed to grow up.

His siblings began to see him as inferior, not because he was younger, but because he was treated in ways that made him feel younger. Emotionally handicapped, he had to find ways to cope with his fears and self-doubts.

No Applause for Peter

Peter was never abused physically, but the scars of his emotional abuse were deep. He tried to be the person his mother wanted him to be. He would soak his pillow wet night after night crying and praying, *Please God, make me good like my brothers. Make me the kind of person my Mama wants me to be.* (Isn't it fortunate that God does not answer all our prayers?) As Peter grew older, his brothers seemed to excel in everything they did, in sports, music, academics. They were the Johnson family superstars. If awards were given they were on stage to receive them, as their parents stood by to applaud their efforts and Peter stood in the wings wishing he could be part of the celebration. But he was still the baby in the family. Since he had no friend at home, Peter found friends in the kitchen cupboard, the refrigerator, the corner store, the snack stand at the movies, in candy bars, ice cream, potato chips, in sandwiches piled high with lunch meats and drowned in salad dressing and mayonnaise.

Peter had found food, and he made food his intimate friend. He had never learned to develop healthy relationships with his parents, his brothers, or other males or females. But food? That was something different. Food was readily accessible, it did not judge him, it made him feel good and, most important, Peter felt he was finally in control of his life. Peter got very large.

Diets create an obsession with food.
Diets provide inadequate nutrition.
Diets don't work!

Years later when he sought help, Peter reflected, "I guess I became large so I'd finally get some attention from my family. If I was going to be a baby I was going to be the biggest, most noticeable, most attention-deserving baby on the block." All Peter wanted was to be noticed by those who said they loved him. And they did. But every member of his family focused on his weight, not on the loving, caring person he had become. He was once the invisible baby; now he had become a very visible young adult who needed fixing. He was seen as a boy who needed lots of diets to make him whole.

The Pain

Peter went back to square one. He found that he had chosen a "safe" way to escape pain. Instead of drugs or alcohol, he numbed his pain with food—one mouthful at a time. As with many addictions, the choice of food for "self-medication" started out innocently enough. After all, what's the danger of a few extra pieces of pie and scoops of ice cream, a couple of donuts on the patio after church, a few extra helpings of potatoes and gravy each night at dinner, and a bag or two of potato chips while watching television?

Being thin doesn't guarantee happiness, and being overweight will not necessarily result in having a poor self-concept. What matters most is how much key people in your life emphasized your appearance as a youngster.

The problem is not the occasional misuse of food, but the misuse of food as "medication" for deeper issues day after day after day. Peter did not know that the crunchy foods he was eating—like potato chips and pretzels—actually promoted uncontrolled eating. Nor did he know of the research that now suggests the crunching sound and jaw action of eating such foods has a stress-relieving effect.

Here's the point. If we, like Peter, do not deal in a straightforward manner with the inner pain we feel, we will somehow find a way to numb it, and in many cases that personally prescribed "drug" will be food. We may use food initially to control our problems, but later food begins to control us. (See appendix 1 for further information on the topic of addition.)

Why Food?

Food is universal. From infancy we learn that food is a source of comfort. It gives us the warmth, physical nourishment, and acceptance we crave as we begin life's journey. Because eating is an oral experience—and a pleasant one at that—in later years if our basic needs are not met we may tend to gratify ourselves with even more of these oral experiences, through food, smoking, chewing our nails, or putting our hands in our mouths excessively. We may move toward even more extreme obsessive-compulsive behavior, an issue I discuss in great length in *Healing the Scars of Emotional Abuse*. Food is a natural, universal, and self-defeating way of dealing with unmet needs.

But we all have to eat. That's why I encourage people to look at eating food as an art, not just something to mask pain. People who lose weight permanently learn to develop a new relationship with food. They do not set out to do this with a rigid set of rules. They've already tried that with diets and failed. What we're talking about is how to help you deal with low impulse control, and how you use food as a weapon in a battle you cannot win. An overweight person's relationship with food needs to become an art that can be learned. An overweight person can learn that no artificial structures such as diets are needed to lose weight permanently.

Three Things to Do

People who lose weight permanently take the time to re-lay the foundations of their lives by dealing with their obsessive-compulsive behavior. With the help of a book like this, counseling, and the affirmation of friends, they learn that:

1. *They're not alone.* They are not islands of pain in an ocean of happiness. Pain is everywhere. No one is immune from sadness or grief. Everyone carries a burden. They discover that there are many people who are ready and able to empathize with them and work at understanding what they are going through.
2. *They have a need to be accepted.* To be accepted means to be taken seriously—something that usually does not happen to us when we're small. People who lose weight permanently learn to ask for what they need, because they know if they don't get what they need they will head to the refrigerator to get what they think they need.
3. *They need to have someone affirm them.* We all need to know that the character we play on the stage of life

has significance, that we are here for a purpose. Nothing is more painful than to be unnoticed, unrecognized, and unaffirmed. Each of us needs to learn the amazing truth that we are important, and this has nothing to do with the size of our clothing or where we are on the journey to permanent weight loss.

How Do You Rate Yourself?

Everything you have tried up to this point has not worked. Diets have not worked, powders have not worked, diet pills have not worked, obsessive exercising has not worked. Every method of weight loss has been flawed. Each has promised you something it could not deliver. That's why it's time to ask yourself some personal questions.

On the following quiz, grade each statement on a score of 1-5. If it's true for you almost all the time, give yourself a 5. If you usually do it, score a 4. If you seldom do it, score a 1. If you never do it, record a 0.

1. I have to be on a diet all the time _____
2. I feel guilty when I eat a dessert _____
3. I wake up thinking about food _____
4. I dream about my weight and/or food _____
5. At parties, I hang around the snack table _____
6. I am ashamed of my body _____
7. I feel it's wasteful if I don't clean my plate _____
8. I seldom sit down to eat _____
9. At buffets, I feel I must try a bit of everything _____
10. I skip breakfast _____
11. I often eat the leftovers after a party at my home _____
12. I am afraid of losing control with food _____
13. I eat most of the cookies I bake while they
    are still warm _____

14. I buy popcorn at the movies even if I've
    just eaten   ____
15. There are only a few safe foods I feel I can eat ____
16. When I'm bored, I get out the snack food   ____
17. I can gain weight overnight   ____

How did you rate yourself? Do you see a pattern? If you had
a total score of 65 or more, I am especially glad you are
reading this book, because there is hope in these pages for
you. If your score was around 50, then you may or may not
need to take action. If your total score was under 25, congratulations. I can only assume you are reading this book so
you can refer it to a friend.

Obsession with Food

Sometimes I think the reason we eat by candlelight is because
we have elevated food to a cathedral-like religious experience.
Our "places of worship" are the open-all-night pavillions dedicated to the sale of fat, calories, and cholesterol, and the eat-
all-you-can-eat troughs of food consumed by people for whom
three full plates are never enough. Those with food obsessions
believe that . . .

Food is relief from stress
Food is reward for pain
Food is the epitome of success
Food is the wafer and wine for the religion of the obese
Food is comfort in a time of storm
Food is life!

When people with eating disorders come to see me I ask them
how much time they think about food. They often say "about
110 percent of the time." That's one of the most honest

statements they'll ever make during treatment. They do spend the majority of the time thinking about food: about when they are or are not going to eat, what they are or aren't going to eat, and where they are or are not going to eat. But the feelings of control these individuals think they have are nothing but a fraud. In fact, the eating disorder is controlling them, consuming their relationships, ruining their self-esteem, destroying their health, and wasting their time. Since you are reading this book, I can only assume you are now becoming aware that your attempts to control food are failing to control the pain, the anger, and the fear you feel.

Recovery Will Keep You Busy

By now you may be ready to admit that food is not—and has never been—your problem. It's something deeper, something you have not addressed, not admitted, not dealt with. Well, if you are now ready to make a move in the right direction, then you are ready to work with the following checklist for recovery as you move from using food to self-medicate your pain to looking at eating as an art. I encourage you to begin to do the following:

- *Learn to be free* in expressing what you believe about yourself and the rigid set of rules you have chosen to live by up until now.

- *Find a safe place*—or a safe person—to begin breaking your formal rules for survival. One of your greatest stressors may be hanging onto the rules made by people in your past. If it is a parental issue, you may want to talk it over with a portrait and tell your mother or father about your new direction. If they are deceased, you may benefit from writing a letter and reading it standing near their graves. Can you imagine your parents affirming your new direction and cheering you on? Start breaking old, ineffective, untrue rules now.

■ *Express yourself* to people who believe in you and have your best interests at heart. These may be people in a social club, book discussion group, a parent or other family member, or perhaps a special neighbor. Determine who can be trusted. When you find such a person, open yourself up little by little.

■ *Quit taking the blame* for all the stuff that's gone on in your life. You are only one actor on a great stage filled with many actors in elaborate costumes (which include masks) who speak both provocative and confounding dialogue. These people have come and gone across the stage of your life. You didn't write the play. (Your parents didn't even write it.) You're not directing the play. In fact, you didn't even ask to be in the play. So don't assume that you are responsible for the play. The only part in the production for which you are responsible is you.

■ *Associate with emotionally healthy people* as often as possible. Believe the words of the old song that exhorts us to "accentuate the positive." Some of us do not have great models of emotional stability in our pasts. It's okay. Now you have a choice between ineffective models and effective ones. Identify with emotionally healthy people, observe them, notice how they deal with people, conflict, and ideas. Spend as much time with them as possible.

■ *Develop good relationship skills.* Starting today, learn:
To ask for help when you need it most
To express your anger in ways that do not hurt others
To ask for what you want (just like you do when you go to a store)

To share yourself with others by doing deeds of kindness
To tell someone when he or she has hurt or disappointed
    you

Earnest Hemingway once wrote, "The world breaks everyone, and afterward many are strong at the broken places." In that same vein, what the slimy caterpillar calls doomsday is what we eventually see as an exquisite butterfly. We all get broken. At some time in our lives each of us slips into the dark cocoon of night, thinking we have little or no hope. But if we choose not to give up, we find there is joy in the morning. What was ugly becomes a thing of beauty.

This is what people who lose weight permanently have come to expect from their lives. They live with hope. They don't deny the past; they deal with it. They make no rigid rules for future growth, they just grow. They are also people who have an attitude of gratitude and are able to speak—and live—the words of this credo:

A Credo of Gratitude

The joy of a life under control is my birthright. To feel this deep inner joy to its edges gives me renewed energy and allows me to rise to the challenges of joining the two percent of people who lose weight permanently. My life has been one of tempests, emotional earthquakes, and shattered dreams. I know I will never be immune from life's pain. But I no longer rely on food for nurture, because I am no longer a hostage of food. Today, and every day of my new life, my thoughts are tied to reality: real joy, real pain, real conflict, real progress. I am more relaxed now, a freer spirit. No longer am I traveling with boxes of bandages, splints, and a much-used parachute, anticipating disaster at every turn. I am taking the risk of believing in my dreams. A comfortable course of action will keep me on the path to permanent weight loss. I am receiving what I desire and am becoming the person God created me to be. For all this and more, I give thanks.

Science and psychology both remind us that the brain cannot make a clear distinction between an established fact and a dominant desire. Therefore, as you repeat aloud the above credo you are telling your brain what you are in the process of becoming: a thankful person who is losing weight permanently. You see yourself as successful. In your mind's eye you have already arrived at your desired goal.

You also know you are not yet there in reality. However, unless you see yourself as complete, whole, loving, joyous, and lovable, your goal of permanent weight loss will be elusive. The saying "Rome wasn't built in a day" is rendered into Chinese as, "A fat person did not get there with one bite." Same message. It takes time to gain, and it takes time to lose. But time is on your side. Besides, being thin does not guarantee you'll be satisfied with your body shape, nor does being a few pounds overweight suggest a poor self-concept. What matters most, according to several studies, is how much your parents, relatives, and those closest to you emphasized your appearance as a child. Now, as one who is losing weight permanently, you know the past is past and the present is now. Whatever was done is done; whatever was said was said. The sooner you quit focusing on your body (or what ancient history may have said about it) the sooner you'll make quality time available for important things in your life.

One of my patients, Rebecca, wrote in her journal of how one day the light went on as she started doing what the two percent do to lose weight permanently. With her permission I share her thoughts with you.

Dr. Jantz pointed out to me that my self-worth at one time was based entirely on what I looked like. If I was thin and attractive, I felt acceptance from myself and others. It seemed so much easier to focus on my appearance, on my outside. My insides were so out of kilter anyway that I couldn't even think about them. If I focused on my body, my weight, food, purging, and exercising, then I didn't have to think about what was wrong with me.

> When I realized how anger, fear, and guilt had contributed to my eating disorder . . . I was finally able to get off that endless merry-go-round.

I didn't understand what was happening to me because the pain was so hard to face. It wasn't until I was in a safe place, with people I felt secure with who knew how to help me, that I could unlock that pain, take a look at it, and reveal the truth.

Understanding the reasons for my behavior has helped me to deal with the guilt I felt all those lost years. It has helped me to deal with the guilt I felt over being a "bad" little girl, with the fear that people wouldn't accept me unless I was thin. When I finally realized how anger, fear, and guilt contributed to my eating disorder, and how my eating disorder had numbed my anger, I was finally able to get off that endless merry-go-round of eating disorders. But it not only helped me. I also began to understand the weight challenges of my ten-year-old daughter. For that insight alone, I thank God.

Rebecca made progress by taking one step at a time toward her goals. One of the first things she did was change her attitude towards what she ate. Here are some steps you can take to change the way you view food.

Action Plan #3

The Art of Making Eating an Art

1. In each of the three boxes below or on a separate piece of paper, write one of your greatest fears.

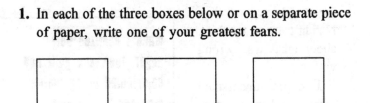

   High impulse control is the ability to keep yourself in touch with reality and not be controlled by your fears. Based on what you've read in this chapter, what do you think will happen to you when you become free and are no longer controlled by fears or anxieties?

2. What specifically can you do to reduce your fears by at least ten percent this week?

3. This diagram shows a portion of your journey in life. It contains seven "minefields" related to food that are waiting to explode if you step on them. Identify these hazardous places and jot down briefly how you will avoid triggering these explosive devices.

Life's Minefields—the hazardous places in your journey

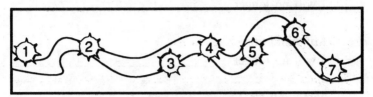

The minefields in my journey of life:

1:

2:

3:

4:

5:

6:

7:

How you will respond:
Minefield #1:
I will no longer _____

Minefield #2:
I will no longer _____

Minefield #3:
I will no longer _____

Minefield #4:
I will no longer _____

Minefield #5:
I will no longer _____

Minefield #6:
I will no longer _____

Minefield #7
I will no longer _____

4. Map out three days of how you could misuse and abuse food. Be creative with this exercise, to the point of being ridiculous. (Then go immediately to #5.)

Day 1

Day 2

Day 3

5. Map out those same three days with specific ideas to show how you will behave now that eating is for you an art rather than an obsession.
Day 1

Day 2

Day 3

Harold Kushner wrote, "When people are loving, brave, truthful, charitable, God is present." Robert Louis Stevenson cautioned us to "sit loosely in the saddle of life." The sentiments of these writers have been the underlying theme of this chapter on making eating an art. Nothing much will ever be accomplished until you cultivate and maintain a deep appreciation and love for the special person God made: you. Nor will your life have much lasting satisfaction if you do not share that love and compassion with others. As far as sitting loosely in the saddle of life, well, that pretty much speaks for itself.

People who lose weight permanently not only sit loosely, they also know in which direction their horse is headed. They understand that negative thoughts can rule their lives as obsessively as any addiction. That's why from this day forward you have chosen to be committed to giving yourself over to expressions of hope and joy. Why? Because you have joined the ranks of the two percent who have chosen to pay the price for losing weight permanently.

But we've only just begun our journey together. Now, as you learn to make eating an art, we will take the next step to help you rediscover how to make friends with your body, a discussion that involves probing the intricacies of the dance of sex and weight, the subject of chapter 4.

Notes

1. Lewis B. Smedes, *Forgive and Forget* (San Francisco: Harper & Row, 1984), p. xiii-xv.

4
People who lose weight permanently skip
THE DANCE OF SEX AND WEIGHT

There's a new diet that is supposed to really work. You only get to eat when there's good news.

The headline on the cover screamed: *Take off 5 lbs. fast! Melt away your Thanksgiving binge.* Inside was a full color piece entitled "Celebrity Inspiration . . . How the stars drop five lbs. fast," a holiday feature found in the pages of *Woman's World.* For Shelley Fabares it's a "magic drink" that keeps her at her ideal weight of 118 pounds. Candice Bergen turns to her "Paris plan," a bowl of onion soup for lunch and dinner, and a banana or apple for breakfast. Dolly Parton likes to "juice it up" by enjoying squeezed orange juice for breakfast, papaya juice for lunch, and a glass of apple cider for dinner *for up to five days* to stay at her trim 105 pounds. A subhead tells us that Whitney Houston likes to "binge on eggs," and when Sharon Stone wants to lose a quick five, she sits down to a sumptuous meal of celery and carrots.

These are the quick-fix, lose-five-pounds-fast regimens of just a few of the twelve ravishing women featured in the article. At first glance their methods of attacking fat may seem to be just the ticket for optimum weight management. Who wouldn't want a sure-fire way to lose a fast five pounds? It all seems so right, so okay, so all-American, so *everybody's doing it.* However, what alarms me is one of the captions over the ever so thin, full-color pictures of Dolly Parton, Joan Collins, Cybill Shepherd, and Sharon Stone which reads:

> Lose that holiday weight and look great with diet strategies from the experts: stars who have to look slim for parties, parts and public appearances.[1]

Here's my concern. Marketing their images by appearing voluptuous, trim, and sexy, and latching on to various diets to guarantee their thinness are obviously important for the celebrity women who grace the pages of the magazine. *But for the article to attempt to tie us to their overnight strategies so that we, too, will look good during the holidays—or any other day of the year—is deceptive.* These strategies may or may not work for others. If they do work, they may just be one diet in a string of compulsive gimmicks. If they don't work— and the article makes no promise they will—then they're just one more fad that's been tried and failed. The piece says nothing about looking "healthy" for the holidays, but focuses only on the quickest way to lose five pounds.

The women in the three-page spread are beautiful. They are expensively coifed, gorgeously attired, slim, big-busted, and sexy. What woman *wouldn't* like to have the shape of these Hollywood beauties! But people who lose weight permanently learn to turn the pages fast when they encounter these sirens of weight loss. That's because they are no longer obsessed with their outer beauty, their waist size, how much they eat, when they eat it, their dress measurements, bust size, what they must wear to cover fat, or how many inches of girth they must lose to be presentable at parties or feel good about themselves at public appearances. The pictures in the magazine are pretty, and the headlines are enticing, but the road to permanent weight loss is *not* to follow in the paths of the stars.

Here is a summary of what nineteen-year-old Donna (not her real name) told me in a private session. I share these thoughts with you with her permission:

Every time I went to the supermarket I would buy a copy of the latest tabloid and at least two or three glamour or fitness magazines. Because I had a weight problem, I devoured the pages, desperately searching for the latest diet cure. I would carefully cut out those beautiful bodies, copy their diets and post them on my refrigerator. Then I'd tackle their suggestions one by one: I'd juice for a few days, then I'd starve myself for a while, then I would drink tea for a week, then I'd exercise nonstop to the point of physical and mental exhaustion, and on and on it went. What drove me to keep trying to lose weight was all these beautiful, big-busted, attractive Hollywood models I'd taped to my refrigerator door. I'd made them my idols. If I could only look like them. But nothing ever worked.

I'd lose a couple pounds, look in the mirror and still not be satisfied with the shape of my body, get disgusted with myself, and then go on a binge by opening the refrigerator (refusing to look at the celebrities staring at me from the door) and cleaning out whatever was inside. Then I'd feel guilty, promising myself I would never diet, worship the stars, or binge again, only to find myself two days later back at the same supermarket checkout stand, picking up yet another sensational tabloid and secretly praying, *This time, please, God, make it work. If they can be beautiful, thin, and sexy, so can I.*

It is confessions such as these that tear at my heart, because I hear them day in and day out in both private and group sessions at The Center. These are desperate people who have been hypnotized by the shrill songs of the Madison-Avenue sirens that attempt to create objects of either desire or lust. In

Greek mythology the Sirens sang melodies so beautiful that sailors passing their rocky island were lured to shipwreck and death. At one point, ancient literature tells us, Odysseus ordered his men to stop their ears with beeswax so that they could not hear the Sirens' songs and to tie him to the ship's mast so that he could not swim ashore. Jason and the Argonauts were saved when Orpheus, who accompanied them, played music that was even more enchanting.

It took ropes and beeswax to save these ancient sailors' lives, and it will take an equal amount of commitment to your program of permanent weight loss to help you learn to play music *even more enchanting than the Madison-Avenue sirens of deceit.* The solution is a program that is for you alone, and not one that needs to meet the scrutiny of others. That's why we say . . .

Comparison Is a Fast Track to Misery!

Let's be honest. There is always going to be someone in this world—and in your life—who will be better than you are at something: better looking than you, slimmer than you, with a sweeter or more patient personality than you, with more money than you, smaller hips than you, more friends than you, and the list could go on endlessly. If you want to be miserable, live a life of making comparisons. You simply cannot win. You are who you are, and others are who they are. If you spend your life comparing yourself with others, you:

1. Will become rigid in body and mind
2. Will demand to be in control at all times (and therefore will be out of control much of the time)
3. Will forget to smile
4. Will dwell on what's wrong instead of what's right about you and others

5. Will blame yourself and others for what's not going well in your life
6. Will expect the worst of yourself instead of what's best
7. Will store your anger deep in your gut, and you will be miserable

Instead of being miserable, you can do the opposite of comparing. You can examine yourself and figure out what is right and healthy and acceptable *for you.*

Look at How You've Used Fat for Comfort

I have had the privilege of working with some remarkable people who have faced unspeakable adversity and painful memories to come to grips with their lives in the present. Many have been severely abused—physically, sexually, and emotionally—and have turned to food, and fat, as their constant companion. Unfortunately, their painful past set them up for lives of even more pain. Many were so intent on looking like those thin, sexy vixens in the glamour magazines that they literally started to walk a path leading to personal destruction. For many, their disordered eating became full-blown anorexia or bulimia. It was no longer simply an obsessive compulsion with weight or overeating. It became a matter of life and death.

In virtually every case, people with severe weight problems had forgotten what they wanted from life. Food had eclipsed whatever their dreams or goals might have been. They no longer felt they had a special purpose in this world. They were in such bondage to food that they'd lost all belief in themselves. Their struggle with food had become more important than their health or their relationships. But as they joined the two percent they learned that their problem was not a food problem. It was a self-image problem, a self-esteem problem, a comparison-with-others problem, a quick-fix problem, a no-patience problem, and a hell-bent-for-leather demand for immediate results problem. Each person had to slow down, re-evaluate the facts, and quietly decide that he or she would deliberately change course. Each one had to learn the power of these words of wisdom found in the writings of an anonymous writer:

Slow Me Down, Lord . . .

Slow me down, Lord! Ease the pounding of my heart by the quieting of my mind. Steady my hurried pace with a vision of the eternal reach of time. Give me, amid the confusion of the day, the calmness of the everlasting hills. Break the tensions of my nerves and muscles with the soothing music of the singing streams that still live in my memory.

Help me to know the magical, restoring power of sleep.

Teach me the art of taking minute vacations—of slowing down to look at a flower, to chat with a friend, to pat a dog, to answer a child's question, to read a few lines from a good book.

Remind me each day of the fable of the hare and the tortoise, that I may know that the race is not always to the swift—that there is more to life than increasing its speed. Let me look upward into the branches of the towering oak and know that it grew slowly and well. Slow me down, Lord, and inspire me to send my roots deep into the soil of life's enduring values, that I may grow more surely toward the stars.

These are good words, aren't they? And especially appropriate for those of us who are in a breakneck race to manage our weight by relying on the hype and other external stimuli which surround us. *Slow down.* Don't do anything extreme. It took a while to reach our present condition, and it will take some time to reach a new, more realistic goal. *Slow down.* We don't need Hollywood stars as our models any longer. We don't need the deceit of the tabloid diets to confuse us. We don't need "body sculpting with liposuction for the low cost of only $2950." Nor do we need laser skin resurfacing to "regain our youthful appearance." We need not sign up for the latest cosmetic procedures called "soft tissue shaving" that call for "less bruising and minimal bleeding."

Good Self-Image

If you hate your body, you will continually move toward behaviors that are self-destructive, be it with food, relationships, personal care, lack of exercise, or poor nutrition. If this self-hatred continues, you will perpetually do things to damage yourself and your self-esteem. But a healthy esteem = a healthy body image. People with healthy self-esteem do not *have* to look like the women in the magazine ads to like themselves. Such people no longer need to be like the pumped up, filled out, muscle-bound body builders in the fitness magazines to feel good about themselves. They know they do not have the perfect body *and it no longer matters*. What counts is that they can now say: I like me as I am. I'm going to make some changes, but I like me in the meantime. They echo the words screened on a T-shirt: *I may not be perfect, but parts of me are excellent.*

Let's do a quick survey. I want you to write down seven things you do NOT like about your body. Write them down quickly in the blanks provided. Do it now.

SEVEN THINGS I DO NOT LIKE ABOUT MY BODY

1. I don't like my _____ because
   _____.

2. I don't like my _____ because
   _____.

3. I don't like my _____ because
   _____.

4. I don't like my _____ because
   _____.

5. I don't like my _____ because
   _____.

6. I don't like my _____ because
   _____.

7. I don't like my _____ because
   _____.

Review what you've written. Dwell on them. Think of them in the extreme. You may have thought your big toe was too big, your hips too wide, your nose too large, or your eyebrows too bushy. Whatever you put down, now say out loud, "So what! Big deal! _____, [your name] are you going to let these ridiculous dislikes keep you from becoming the person you want to be?" Here's the problem: The more you focus on individual blemishes on your body, the more you distort your body as a whole; the more you rivet your attention on what is not perfect, the more you expand your disdain for your body; and the more you hate your body, the more susceptible you become to the deceit of the glamour magazines.

Now, let's do just the opposite. Write down seven things you *do* like about your body. Write them down quickly in the blanks provided. Do it now.

SEVEN THINGS I LIKE ABOUT MY BODY

1. I like my _____ because
   _____.

2. I like my _____ because
   _____.

3. I like my _____ because
_____.

4. I like my _____ because
_____.

5. I like my _____ because
_____.

6. I like my _____ because
_____.

7. I like my _____ because
_____.

How would you compare these two exercises? Was one easier for you to complete than the other? In what way? Now focus only on the above seven blanks you've just completed. Read each one slowly and carefully. Look at yourself in a mirror, if possible, as you read each one aloud. You may have said, "I like my ears because they know how to listen." Or, "I like my fingers because they are long and artistic." Now ask yourself these questions: How do I *feel* about myself as I compare what I've written in the two exercises? When I speak *negatively* of my body, does it make me feel good, helpful, and cause me to want my dreams to come true? What about when I speak in *positive* terms of my body? How do I feel about *me* when I take the time to be grateful for what God has given me—perfect or

Whenever you make any major change, others will—intentionally or not—try to get you to change back. This is not something to fear, but to welcome as another opportunity for growth. Others may be more comfortable with you the way you were.

not? Do I feel my spirits lift? When I express appreciation for what I have, does this make me feel better about myself?

The Subconscious Mind

Learning not to compare and not to use glamour magazines as your measure of success brings emotional health of the highest order. The philosopher José Ortega y Gassett once wrote, "Tell me to what you pay attention, and I will tell you who you are." You are *not* food. You are not a diet. You are you, a unique person created in the image of a loving God. You are not what you think you are, but what you *think*, you are.

The subconscious mind never stops working, never gets tired, and never says *no* to any input it receives from you. It believes everything it hears and trusts everything you say or feel. It even responds to your most innocent thoughts, especially those thoughts which are highly emotionalized with either faith or fear. It is even more susceptible to repetitive thoughts. (Remember: "Tell me to what you pay attention, and I will tell you who you are.")

That's why daily affirmations are so effective. Your mind cannot distinguish fact from desire.

TWO AFFIRMATIONS:

I can lose all the weight I want, and still keep my cherished values.

I now believe that weight loss = power = sexual energy = fear + guilt, BUT emotional health = weight loss = physical vitality.

When you say, "I care about myself, and I am becoming the person I was meant to be; I like what God has created, *and* I am a person who is losing weight permanently," then a wonderful world of self-acceptance begins to unfold. The book of ancient wisdom reminds us that as a person thinks in his heart, so he is. That's a very old saying, but no less true today than when it was written. Think good thoughts of yourself. Never put yourself down. What you think, *you are*. Your subconscious hears *it* all and believes *it* all. Treat it with respect. It is one of the most important parts of something called *you*.

Dealing with Success

You now should be aware that food is not the problem for you. It never has been, and it never will be the problem. As this thought becomes more imbedded in the chapters that follow, you will begin to recognize just how close you really are to your objective of permanent weight loss. But for every action there will be a reaction, and here is where some will fall off the wagon and revert to older, ineffective behavioral patterns.

■ Suppose you're a woman who's now lost ten or twenty pounds. You are trim, you're feeling great, you walk with more spring in your step, you feel more confident than ever and then *Whaam!* A handsome coworker—who never paid much attention to you before—now detains you at the office water cooler and begins to express some interest in you. Scary, perhaps. When you were carrying around those extra pounds you did not have to deal with the attention of men. In fact, you may have put on weight in the past so men would *not* seek you out. Now what do you do? Run? Seek cover? Or will you learn to *trust yourself* with your weight loss? This is a very important issue for you to prepare for because you may feel as if you have a new body and not know how to respond to the attention. In fact you *do* have a new body. You are going through a significant transformation.

■ What happens if you lose weight and your spouse suddenly begins treating you differently—good or bad? What are your greatest fears?

■ What happens if you become so attractive you are literally scared to death? Some women I've worked with are afraid of being raped, so they've shielded their bodies with weight all their lives.

It's possible that your fears may suddenly become quite extreme, and as your fear goes up, so may your weight. That's often how it works. But it doesn't have to be that way for you. That's why there are at least three critical levels of fortification that must occur for you along the way:

1. Don't lose weight in anger. It will short-circuit your progress. If someone says to you, "Gee, you're looking nice. Have you lost weight?" it's easy for you to hear those words as a put-down. Instead, reframe them. Say to yourself, *If he only knew what was really going on. Yes, I've lost weight, but that's only a byproduct of other, more important things I'm dealing with.* Remind yourself that you're now dealing with your success, not living with former failure.

2. Say good-bye to resentment. As you join the two percent who lose weight permanently, the intensity of your emotions may increase to the level where you may feel you are more out of control than in the past. Further, you'll need to remember that you have *no control* over how others will respond to you as you lose weight. Some will be rude: "Lost your double chin, eh?" "What's the matter, no more french fries and malts with the girls anymore?" "Wow, you must have really had a weight problem, because you look so good now." Remember, some people will not know what to say to you. So you'll need to learn to take care of yourself while caring for others. It's not going to be easy, but it is the permanent attitude of people who lose weight permanently.

3. No hermit's life for you. Your previous weight problem was simply an outward manifestation of other emotional challenges which you are now dealing with from a fresh perspective. You've made great progress, so stay with the program. You want the opposite of a hermit's life. You're working for an integration of the total you: body, soul, and spirit. You need to join in, not separate yourself. As you learn to deal successfully and effectively with your success, your self-esteem will rise and your self-confidence will carry you on. It will not necessarily be easy, but the reward will be a thousand times greater than the effort.

Victim No More

I mentioned earlier in this chapter that many who have weight challenges have been abused in one way or another: not all, but a vast majority. You may be such a person, yet you may never have dealt with the issue because of the emotional trauma you feared it might release. However, I encourage you to take a look at your past and be as honest as you can with yourself. If the word *abuse* is too strong, or even inappropriate for you, then I would like you to substitute the word *victim,* because most weight problems have as their backdrop some form of victimization. You may have suffered emotional put-downs, physical beatings, sexual assaults, perpetual rudeness by a family member, or lack of moral support—the "You'll never amount to anything" kind of statements. All those feelings you still have about those events *will have an effect* on how you view food. That's why it's important for you to relive them momentarily, even if this is painful. To help you do this, indicate in each column when you were victimized, in what particular setting, how often, and your response *today* to what happened in the past.

INSTANCES OF ABUSE OR VICTIMIZATION

When? How Often? My Response
1. Financially _____
2. Workplace _____
3. Community service group _____
4. School _____
5. Relatives _____
6. Friends _____
7. Church setting _____
8. Sports _____
9. Miscellaneous _____

As you look over your comments you may say, "There's not much to do with weight here." Actually, it may be *all* about weight, because people who lose weight permanently have had to deal with some form of abuse or victimization. Sometimes they brought it upon themselves, but often it was a product of their youth. If you have been a time bomb ready to explode, free floating, and loaded with unresolved anger or guilt from the past, there's no telling what you may have done. One thing we can assume, however, is that you have been living a life that's out of control. That's why you're reading this book. You want to regain control of your life. You want optimum health. You want emotional stability. You want to be filled with physical energy that defines a person who's one hundred percent alive. The fascinating contradiction is this: It's *all about* weight and *none of it* is about weight.

Now you are taking your motivation for living in a new direction. You are no longer living with unresolved issues of anger, fear, hurt, and guilt. You are now on the threshold of using your God-given energy to become a complete, whole person who knows you can join the two percent who lose weight permanently. You have finally discovered some great purposes for your life. You've crawled out of the box marked "victim of the past" and have stepped boldly into the rarefied air of emotional freedom.

You may have started reading this book thinking you would have *to do something* specific—like pursue a plan—to lose weight permanently. Now you know that weight loss is only a by-product of your commitment to becoming a more emotionally healthy you. No longer will you dance the dance of weight and sex. The sexy, picture-perfect models, the hype advertisements that promote cosmetic tinkering, and the deceit of fad diets are no longer even options for you. You have turned a corner. You are on your way to joining the two percent who succeed in losing weight permanently. To help move you even further along your way, I urge you to complete the following action plan now.

Action Plan #4

Just Say No to the Dance of Sex and Weight

1. There are many common elements that occur in a family where victimization takes place. You may not have experienced all—or even most—of the following, but check all statements that come close to what you remember as a child. Even if this proves to be a difficult exercise, I encourage you to do it now.

   ____ There were many broken promises.
   ____ I was verbally abused as a child.

_____In my family there was "emotional incest" where family members communicated inappropriate sexual messages, even though they never touched me.

_____I had to work hard to get any respect from my family.

_____My father was the king, and the rest of us were treated as subjects.

_____We were relatively poor and had little money even for the necessities.

_____I don't remember much about my growing up years. I just don't feel they were a very positive time for me.

_____Jokes were always being made about my body: "Your breasts are too big," or "too small"; "You are too tall," or "too short"; "Your hips are too big," etc.

_____I received lots of spankings. Now, when I look back, it may actually have been borderline abuse.

_____I dressed seductively in the past and am afraid I may do it again.

_____I was always afraid that something very frightening was going to happen.

_____I was forced to engage in sexual acts.

2. One of the things that keeps people from emotional growth is unnecessary shame. Before you can really move toward joining those who lose weight permanently, it will be necessary for you to call out your shame for being overweight and recognize it for what it really is. Write your thoughts for each of these statements:

A. I feel ashamed of my weight because my friends:

B. I feel ashamed of my weight because my children:

C. I feel ashamed of my weight because my boss at work:

D. I feel ashamed of my weight because my spouse/relatives:

E. I feel ashamed of my _____ (specific body part) because _____.

3. Now that you are looking at many of the reasons that may have propelled you to gain weight in the past, you know you no longer need to be ashamed of your temporary condition. Now that you are better able to trust yourself—and not revert to feelings of shame—complete the following sentences.

A. Now I can trust myself with my friends because:

B. Now I can trust myself with my boss because:

C. Now I can trust myself with my spouse/relatives because:

D. Now I can trust myself with tabloid articles about crash diets, pictures of beautiful models, etc., because:

4. Make a list of fifteen things in your life for which you are truly grateful. People who lose weight permanently maintain an attitude of gratitude, and this spirit of thankfulness will pull others to you and enrich all your relationships. We now know that the more grateful you are for the good things in your life, the less you will need food as your constant companion.

   a.

   b.

   c.

   d.

   e.

   f.

   g.

   h.

   i.

   j.

k.

l.

m.

n.

o.

5. Call two people on the telephone today and tell them what their friendship means to you.

6. Trust yourself to lose ten pounds now—without diets or weight loss programs. Review all the preceding chapters of this book and simply let yourself begin to implement what we've been learning together. Remember, you no longer need to compare yourself with others to lose weight, because you now know that *comparison is a fast track to misery,* and it will only promote jealousy, envy, and anger. Success is an inside job.

In his landmark book *The Psychology of Winning,* Dr. Denis Waitley reminds us that

Winners "make" it happen. Losers "let" it happen. The true meaning of self-control is often misunderstood. Many people interpret self-control as "getting a good grip on yourself" or remaining cool and passive under pressure. Self-control . . . is synonymous with self-determination. Winners take full responsibility for determining their actions in their own lives. They believe in Cause and Effect, and have the philosophy that life is a "do-it-to-yourself-program." . . . Voltaire likened life to a game of cards. Each player must accept the cards life deals him or her. But once they are in hand, he or she alone must decide how to play the cards in order to win the game. The writer, John Erskine, put it a little differently when he wrote: "Though we sometimes speak of a primrose path, we all know that a bad life is just as difficult, just as full of work, obstacles and hardships, as a good one. *The only choice is the kind of life one would care to spend one's efforts on.*" [Emphasis added][2]

I especially like John Erskine's final words, "The only choice is the kind of life one would care to spend one's efforts on." How are you spending *your efforts?* Are your daily actions taking you in the direction of your dreams? It is my hope and prayer that they are. One certain way to accelerate your journey of permanent weight loss is to disconnect the cycle of past hurt, fear, and guilt, and get out your bicycle for a vigorous, *noncompulsive, no rules* workout—something we all need to get exercised about—in chapter 5.

Notes

1. *Woman's World,* Vol. XVI, No. 48, 28 November 1995, pp. 14-16.

2. Denis Waitley, *The Psychology of Winning* (n.c.: Nightingale-Conant Corp., 1979), pp. 70-71.

5

People who lose weight permanently go

FROM GUILT CYCLE TO BICYCLE

*The only exercise some people get is jumping to
conclusions, running down their friends,
sidestepping responsibility, dodging issues,
passing the buck, and pushing their luck.*

When I met John at one of my eating disorder seminars,
he told me he'd just joined his fourth health club. I
thought perhaps he was doing a survey of the various
gyms in town. Why else would someone join four clubs? But
he was at least one hundred pounds overweight, and I found
in him a pattern I had seen before. John was excited about
the enormous possibilities of his new fitness center. This fat-
burning factory was complete with floor-to-ceiling mirrors, the
latest design of Stairmasters and climbers, a simulated "rock
wall," treadmills, bicycles, racquetball, squash, free weights,
and what seemed like an acre of exercise machines promising
miracles for people with weight problems.

The club also boasted a huge aerobics room where John
told me the pounds would probably start dropping off the moment he completed his first session. According to John, the
club also had the best, most expensive personal trainers in the

area, a juice bar second to none, and a state-of-the-art fitness program that had been proven effective in other areas of the city. On and on he went. He was so enthused about his new-found opportunity to get fit that I thought he must have been one of the investors. He bought some of my books, a few audiotapes, and said he knew all this would help him as he continued on his way to a life of thinness. In fact, he was going to start listening to my tapes on the stationary bicycle first thing Monday.

Four Health Clubs Too Many

I never saw John again. But I did *hear* about him through a friend. I learned that John not only had joined his fourth health club, but that he still belonged to the other three. He just didn't use them. They were too old, needed painting, the equipment wasn't up-to-date enough, there were no juice bars, the trainers were just okay, and besides, parking wasn't all that great— John had to walk too far from his car to the gym. For John, exercise only began when he gave the desk his card, suited up, and got on the machines. No one was more pleased than John when the new fitness center came to town. *Perhaps this one will do the trick,* he thought. *I'm not losing weight any place else, so it must be those other clubs. It can't be my fault. Finally, I've found a gym that will work for me.*

I learned that John had been on nine different diets during the previous two years. His hobby seemed to be looking for and eating specially prepared, expensive packaged diet foods, hoping the next brand would provide the secret to permanent weight loss. Good old John was also a regular at the weekly overeaters support group. And whenever he saw a television campaign for a new diet or diet product, he was among the first to line up at the health food store to try it. While he was there, he always picked up a few new books on dieting, stretching, weight lifting, and vitamins. But the story doesn't stop there.

It's now Friday. John has become a charter member of the new club. He's received his temporary card, has taken the grand tour, and has even met the owners. He feels part of the establishment. He's been accepted. John says he especially likes all the lotions and potions in the men's locker room. "Hey, even if I don't lose a lot of weight I'm sure going to smell good." John made an appointment to start his new fitness program the following Monday. Unfortunately, there's something between Friday and Monday called a *weekend,* and John loves weekends. But this one would be special, a sort of celebration for what he knew would happen on Monday at the crack of dawn with his new trainer. So what do you do when you celebrate? Eat. In fact, you eat a lot. "If I'm going to have a last meal before the big program, it's going to be a large one." So, John binged all weekend, and really ate a lot on Saturday night. In fact, he ate as if there was no tomorrow. "Hey, I owe myself this food, especially if I'm going to deprive myself of what I want to eat in the weeks ahead." But Covert Bailey points out in *The New Fit or Fat:*

> When a naturally skinny person eats 1000 calories, all of them get burned, wasted, or somehow used up. When a fat person eats 1000 calories, perhaps only 900 of them are used up and the remaining 100 are converted to fat. . . . The fat person's body adjusts somehow to the making of excess fat.

Maybe Tomorrow!

It's Monday morning at 6 A.M. The alarm sounds and John hits the snooze button. Guess what? He oversleeps and misses his 7 A.M. appointment with the trainer at his new club. But that's no problem, because trainers are there all day and into the night. So he reschedules for early that evening. He's getting excited now. He's got a new designer tank top, new water bottle, expensive workout shoes, new shorts and a new attitude. Of course he's going to do this. But he forgot he has to work late Monday night, and so he misses his appointment. Besides, there's a PTA meeting at 8 P.M., so it really wouldn't have worked out anyway. And so it goes with John. At last report, he still hadn't met with his trainer, and he was apparently out looking for another gym that had better equipment, a more understanding staff, newer methods of training, and, yes, parking that was closer to the club.

Does this sound familiar? I wish I could tell you I concocted this story. I didn't. John is actually living this kind of unproductive, off-the-wall life, and he's going nowhere fast. Unfortunately, for every John, there are thousands of other men and women like him who are wishing, hoping, and praying that a force outside themselves will magically fix them, help them lose weight, make them feel good about themselves, remove the guilt of not exercising, and provide them with a guaranteed program that will keep them thin forever. Unfortunately, the answer is not in external forces. Permanent weight loss is an inside job, and people who lose weight permanently know it. Those who are willing to look at everything about their lives—and are willing to make the necessary changes—are the two percent who've determined never again to allow external influences to guide their future.

No More Guilt

What are the first three words that come to your mind when you think "exercise?"

1. _____
2. _____
3. _____

What you don't need to join people who lose weight permanently . . .

- **weighted jump rope**
- **resistance ball**
- **water weights**
- **walking shoes**
- **sweat belt**
- **sauna suit**
- **portable stereo**
- **designer sweatshirt**
- **pedometer**

What did you write? Many people would write words like, *boring, time-consuming, expensive.* But when it comes to exercise, the most important questions people ask are, "How can I make exercise fun? What can I do that is so enjoyable that I'll look forward to doing it day after day, week after week, year after year?"

Exercise must be fully compatible with you and your personality. If you hate to run, don't run, because if you hate it, you won't do it. If a sweaty, inconvenient five-day-a-week regimen in a local fitness club is not for you, don't do it. That was John's problem. He'd conned himself into believing that he had to go for a big weight-loss program in a big club, with big fees, big trainers and big, expensive equipment, or do nothing at all. Unfortunately, John chose nothing, and therefore he may never join the two percent who lose weight permanently.

Exercise is not about feeling guilty for what you can't—or choose not to—do. The guiltier you feel, the less exercise you will do, and the less exercise you do, the guiltier you will feel, and your guilt cycle will produce depression, confusion, and anger to the point where your entire system may simply close down. The solution: Do what is right for you. Choose an activity that is fun. For many people, the best initial exercise program is simply to walk. Walking requires no expensive club dues, no unique clothing or special shoes, no time limits, no stop watches, no subscriptions to fitness magazines, no nothing. With walking there are also no excuses. If it's hot, walk early. If it's raining, wear a raincoat or carry an umbrella, then come home and take a hot shower. It's one of the most invigorating feelings ever. Try it. (Note: If you live in Alaska or some other cold clime and it's winter, and you can't walk without freezing your body, you might consider walking in place or riding a stationary bike or doing some push-ups or bouncing for a few minutes each day on a small trampoline.)

> **Make exercise fun: Choose an activity that you really enjoy.**

No Excuses, Please

People who lose weight permanently are realistic, and they make their activity program work for them. Exercise is their slave, not their master. When they walk, they know it directs a hefty supply of oxygen to their lungs, gives them a chance to be away from their busy life for a few moments, helps them think about their progress toward permanent weight loss, gives them a few moments to listen to the birds, smell the flowers, and spend quality time with their spouse, a neighbor, or a friend as they take on the familiar and unfamiliar streets and lanes of their neighborhood.

An exercise you choose to do because it's right for you makes you feel good. Before long you begin to experience a wonderful freedom from depression and guilt. The right kind of exercise—that you choose—can actually put joy back into your life, while diets—or expensive health clubs you join because you feel guilty for not working out—inevitably rob you of your joy. One of the most important things I can say in this chapter is . . .

There are no rules for exercise, absolutely none!

People who lose weight permanently know this. They exercise appropriately, but they do exercise. Some join health clubs and go through unbelievable routines—but they do it according to their own rules. Others just walk a few minutes a day, ride a stationery bike, lift some light weights a few minutes a day as it fits into their schedule. According to a recent Harvard study of some seventeen thousand men, those who did the equivalent of about thirty minutes a day of hard exercise five days a week had death rates up to twenty-five percent lower than those who did nearly nothing. That's the scientific evidence. But it doesn't mean that you have to do it if it's not for you, because it's not the only way to stay healthy—or alive.

A mounting pile of evidence also tells us that if you go far enough—and often enough—walking is as good a path to healthy living as anything you can do. This is normally not casual strolling where you kibitz with your neighbors and stop in for morning coffee. Unless, of course, this is what you choose to do. And if you do, that's okay, too. Remember, there are no hard and fast rules for how you do your activity. One day in the future you may want to maximize your walking by doing three or four miles an hour on a regular basis. Your body will thank you, and over the long haul you will discover increasingly improved health. But it's not a rule that you do this. Only do it if you want to.

Yes, there is scientific evidence that proclaims you must drive your heart rate to at least sixty percent of its maximum for twenty minutes to an hour by running, cycling, or swimming to be in the low-vigorous range. But this may not be right for you now or ever. People who lose weight permanently know that weight loss is about personal freedom and liberation, not a codified set of rules.

Operation Personal Freedom

As you see by now, this book takes a different approach to weight loss. It's not at all about technique, timing, rules, or comparisons. There are other books out there if you are going to take physical fitness to a higher level, books like Covert Bailey's *The New Fit or Fat* and *Smart Exercise*. But for those suffering from extreme weight—who have never been able to get it off and keep it off—I'm convinced that they do better initially without techniques or rules. Nor do they need to suffer the fear of comparing their progress with the success of others. Their pain is already too great. The attacks on their self-esteem are trouble enough.

> **New Guidelines for Exercise**
> 1. I will not buy anything special to get started.
> 2. I will do nothing compulsively.
> 3. I will not engage in any obsessive behavior.

In your heart of hearts ask yourself, *What do I really want in my life? Do I want a body to rival the latest cover girl on my favorite magazine, or do I want happiness and a deep sense of inner joy? Do I really want "buns of steel," or would I be happier with lasting peace of mind and good friends?* You already know that unfulfilled expectations invariably lead to guilt, which leads to depression, which leads to compulsive behavior, which leads to using food for comfort—comfort to get out of the depression, which leads back to anger at ourselves that we did it again! This anger paralyzes us with fear that we're never going to able to do this . . . and the beat goes on.

List three simple physical activities you enjoy and can do easily. Plan to start doing at least one of these today. Schedule it on your calendar:

1. _____

2. _____

3. _____

Only when we dismount our guilt cycle do we give ourselves permission to get on the bicycle, the treadmill, the machines at the club, or simply do a few minutes of nonthreatening activity each day. We are interested in progress, not perfection. God created you with a natural desire to be active, so let's recapture that excitement as you go back to doing some of the things you may have enjoyed as a child. Perhaps it was tennis, swimming, running, hiking in the woods, walking, or a game of softball. You may not want to do those same things today, but you can use your past history as a starting point for your future well-being. Who knows, you may rekindle some excitement for the things you haven't done in years.

There's no need to try to re-live the life of a sixteen-year-old high-school cheerleader. That probably won't work. If you were 103 pounds on the varsity tennis team, and you are now considerably in excess of that, think of the enjoyment of tennis, not your weight. One way to make your activity easier and more fun will be to find partners to play with you. It may be a walking friend, a tennis friend, or a bike friend. Exercise is not necessarily a sweat-it-out-alone situation. It is a relational activity. Find a friend to exercise with you—someone you enjoy being with and with whom you have things in common.

The key is to start your activity today, and never stop! If there is a key, it is that. Just keep on going, a little at a time, always moving in a forward direction and never saying quit. Here's a poem handed to me at one of my recent seminars that may give you the extra push you need to take control of your life and then keep on going.

When things go wrong as they sometimes will,
When the road you're trudging seems all uphill,
When the funds are low and the debts are high
And you want to smile, but you have to sigh,
When care is pressing you down a bit,
Rest! if you must—but never quit.

Life is strange, with its twists and turns,
As every one of us sometimes learns,
And many a failure turns about
When he might have won if he'd stuck it out;
Stick to your task, though the pace seems slow—
You may succeed with one more blow.

Success is failure turned inside out—
The silver tint of the clouds of doubt—

And you never can tell how close you are,
It may be near when it seems afar;
So stick to the fight when you're hardest hit —
It's when things seem worst that YOU MUSTN'T QUIT.
Anonymous

People who lose weight permanently make small, daily steps toward their goal because they know that inch by inch, virtually anything is possible. Once you decide what your activity level will be, I encourage you to simply increase it by ten percent per month. You'll be amazed at your progress within only a few weeks.

10% increase each month in activity level

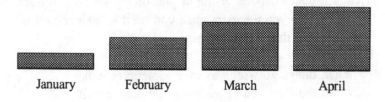

| January | February | March | April |

Once you make this commitment to increase your activity level slowly and gently, you will find you've made a major paradigm shift from compulsive exercising, where exercise is the master, to where you and you alone are in control. Once you decide which activity you choose to do, then you will do it, because you decided. If you do not enjoy it, your activity will become a duty, which will lead to guilt, depression, anger, and ultimately fear. And we are not into fear. Try using the following affirmations by reading them aloud two to three times a day or more. They are your ticket to reshaping your mind-set as you reshape your body in a natural, pleasing, effective way. You can photocopy this page of the book and cut up the affirmations to make cards or rewrite the statements onto 3 x 5 cards. The Center also has more affirmation cards available, so you can contact us at the address in the back of the book.

AFFIRMATIONS

1. God made me an active and alive human being. I am enthusiastically believing this as I enjoy my life to its fullest.
2. My body was created to move, not sit still. That's why I engage in one activity at least fifteen minutes a day. I am happy there are no rules for this activity.
3. I am excited about my balanced schedule of activity. I feel good about myself just knowing that I'm making progress.
4. I'm delighted that I can be active without weighing myself. The scale used to be my judge, jury, and executioner. Now I simply enjoy life.
5. I now know that permanent weight loss is an inside job. I make no demands of my exercise routine. It's simply an important part of maintaining my emotionally healthy life.
6. I believe the words of the ancient prophet Jeremiah who said, "For I know the plans I have for you . . . they are plans for good and not for evil to give you *a future and a hope.*" I believe this with all my heart and soul.
7. I have made a decision to join the growing ranks of people who lose weight permanently. I am increasing my activity level ten percent each month, and my body is responding with a resounding THANK YOU!
8. My attitude is my choice. I can enjoy my daily activity for its sheer enjoyment. I am choosing a healthy, positive attitude about my daily success.

If you're still avoiding starting to exercise, look over these twenty questions. A yes to more than five of the following means you have an eating problem.

TWENTY QUESTIONS

1. Have I ever been so discouraged about my weight that I've just thrown up my hands in despair?
2. Have I ever panicked when I knew I'd be away from food for a while—while on a trip or stuck in rush hour traffic?
3. Do I eat for reasons other than being hungry—like when I'm mad that my team lost, or during commercials on television, or when I'm anxious?
4. Do I suspect that people talk disparagingly about me behind my back?
5. Do I avoid putting myself in new situations because of my weight?
6. Do I sometimes lie about my weight?
7. When I watch a diet or exercise equipment infomercial on television, do I think about how I can buy the products by using another account so my spouse won't know I bought them?
8. Is my negative thinking about myself keeping me from seeing life in general in a positive light?
9. Do I talk a lot about food, read about food, buy recipe books, and generally think food is more exciting than the invention of the telephone?
10. Do I sometimes automatically give in to the server in a restaurant when the tray of desserts comes to my table?
11. Do I avoid looking at my reflection in store windows?
12. At a party, do I spend time grazing at the snack table, eating all the nuts, candies, potato chips and dips, assuming that the carrots and celery are only there for people who enjoy making noises with their mouths?

13. Do I feel bad about myself when I'm with thin people, thinking that if I just dieted more I could be like them?

14. Do I hoard food as if I expected the supermarket employees to go on strike at any moment?

15. When I find a half-price ad for a new fitness center in town, instead of tearing it out, do I tear it up because it hurts too much to look at it?

16. Do I feel I need to cook fattening, high-calorie, gourmet meals for my family, rather than simple, healthy dishes?

17. Have I either heard—or told my children—that we should clean our plates because there are hungry children overseas?

18. Would I love to take a dance class at Arthur Murray, but fear not even the instructor could get his arms around me?

19. Do I know I need to exercise, not only to help me lose weight, but for my own sense of well-being, but I just can't take the first step?

20. When I watch television am I grateful for six commercials in a row so I can go into the kitchen and load up on more food?

When a person is overweight, it's easy to believe that everything one attempts may end in failure. Because of some early, unhappy experiences, a person may tend to exaggerate the negative and assume the consequences of any new behavior will be too painful to try. If such doubts lurk in your mind, now is the hour to begin to turn the tide in your own thinking. When you find yourself thinking, *It's impossible,* stop and ask, *Are these thoughts based on current fact or old programming?* Are you prepared to be ruled by your fears, or are you going to take steps toward personal freedom?

The good news is that you already have the courage to do what you need to do. You don't need to wait for a better time to start your daily, fifteen-minute activity. No time is better than now to make your decision to take action. You don't need better equipment, better weather conditions, better food, better clothes, better friends, better instruction manuals, better affirmations, or better counseling for you to get better. Just get moving! It's what the two percent do who succeed in losing weight permanently. They just start moving—and never quit!

Your new activity will do wonders for your body and for the way you feel about your body. Ninety percent of those who come to me for weight counseling tell me that even the simplest form of activity has helped them feel better about themselves, and that weight loss—which was once their focus—has actually become a by-product of their renewed sense of self-esteem. What's amazing is that, before long, they find themselves indulging in small, sensual pleasures, such as soaking in scented baths, getting massages, taking romantic trips, and wearing silk—things that never would have happened when they viewed themselves as fat, unlovely, and unlovable. Your new activity may do this for you. People who lose weight permanently no longer spend their time thinking about food, their bodies, exercise, competition, or comparing their progress with others. Their new, liberated mind-set gives them—as it will give you—the time to do the really important things in life!

Inspiration for Your Journey to Health

Before you put this chapter to work by giving your responses to the Action Plan, here are some quotes to help you move another step closer to joining the two percent who lose weight permanently:

> Great works are performed not by strength, but by perseverance.—*Samuel Johnson*

If you stay committed, your dreams can come true. I'm living proof of it. I left home at seventeen and had nothing but rejections for twenty-five years. I wrote more than twenty screenplays, but I never gave up. —*Michael Black, author of* Dances with Wolves

Success seems to be connected with action. Successful people keep moving. They make mistakes, but they don't quit.—*Conrad Hilton*

Real courage is when you know you're licked before you begin, but you begin anyway and see it through no matter what.—*Harper Lee*

I skate where the puck is going to be, not where it has been.—*Wayne Gretzky*

(Now I'd like you to write your own inspirational, motivational, quotable quote based on what you've gleaned from this chapter and then mail it to me at P.O. Box 700, Edmonds, WA 98020. I would like to use it when speaking and in future writings, with your permission.)

Action Plan #5

From Guilt Cycle to Bicycle

1. Write your response to this comment by General Omar Bradley: "Bravery is the capacity to perform properly even when scared half to death." What frightens you about taking the first tentative steps toward a regular activity? Can you relate to Bradley's comment?

2. Put yourself in this position. You are a weight-loss counselor. A client comes to you for help. You share how people who lose weight permanently succeed, but specifically you speak of the importance of moving away from guilt for not exercising to the joy and freedom that comes from some kind of enjoyable activity. What would be your three main points?

Point a:

Point b:

Point c:

3. What do the following four concepts mean to you?

Free to risk:

Free to change:

Free to trust:

Free to love and accept:

4. "If it is to be, it's up to me!" Here's what I'm prepared to do—starting today—to create my own activity program:

The Nobel Prize-winning physician Albert Szent-Gyorgyi defined creative thinking: "Discovery consists in looking at the same thing as everyone else and thinking something different." I think you can do that.

6
People who lose weight permanently adopt

A NUTRITIONAL PLAN THAT REALLY WORKS

Take good care of your body. It's the only place you have to live.
Jim Rohn

H ere is a remarkable story told in the words of the person who lived it:

My name is Sally. If I had told you two years ago about my thirteen diets, the more than one hundred bottles of diet pills I'd consumed, my constant bingeing, and the way I hid food in the garage, closets, and the attic, I would have spoken to you as a woman without hope. I'd tried everything under the sun to lose weight, and nothing worked. Absolutely nothing. Two years ago I was thirty-two years old and was eighty-five pounds overweight. At one point I weighed as much as 253 pounds. I was a very large woman. Whenever I'd look at my high school yearbook and see a picture of the slim 103-pound Sally, I would cry, truly believing I would never be thin again. I was convinced there was no hope for me. I don't care what people say, but *fat people are not all jolly.* Most of us are miserable. I was obese. I hated myself and everything about me. My marriage was in ruins, my children didn't want to be seen in the same zip code with me, and my few friends were becoming fewer every day.

If I hadn't been such a coward I might have ended it all. But down deep there was a faint spark of hope that there might be something I had not yet tried that would be the key to unlock the prison door that kept me in bondage. I discovered the *key* to be something I'd never considered in my entire life.

You Are What You Eat!
• In 1994, the average American consumed almost 22 pounds of salt snacks—pretzels, potato chips, popcorn, and cheese puffs—a 4-pound increase over 1988. The amount spent per person on these munchies: $57.10.
• The five most common orders in restaurants in 1994 were carbonated beverages, french fries, hamburgers, pizzas, and side salads.
• The average American consumes nearly 30 pounds of hamburger per year.
• About a third of all vegetables Americans eat are white potatoes.[1]

I could have lectured on the different kinds of diets and schemes available to the consumer today because I feel as if I've done them all. I was proficient at counting calories to the point of obsession. I could *look* at a food in the supermarket from ten feet away and tell you how many calories it contained. I was very good. I'd also become an expert on packaged diet foods and could have spoken with great knowledge about how and why they worked, quoting word for word the testimonials of the celebrities who endorsed them. I would watch—and even videotape for future viewing—the late-night infomercials, each one touting a new diet, an advanced easy-to-do exercise program, a new state-of-the-art piece of equipment that was allegedly the most scientifically created and designed to help me lose weight and keep it off. I had so much knowledge about weight loss that I would often surprise myself, thinking, *Sally, if you have all this information, why are you still over two hundred pounds? What are you NOT doing right? Is it really in your genes? Do you have deficient DNA? Perhaps you will always be fat, Sally; go ahead and be realistic. You'll never change.*

One day, out of desperation, I made a phone call to The Center for an appointment. I really didn't think much would come of it, because I'd made those kinds of calls many times before. But I was coming to the end of the line. I don't remember much about that first session, but I do recall hearing one thing that blew my mind: People who lose weight permanently do not count things.

This is ridiculous, I thought. *How can I lose weight if I don't know how many calories there are in the food or product?* The next bombshell I heard was that I no longer needed to weigh myself. *Nonsense. This kind of counseling is simply not going to fly.* Weighing myself had been a ritual since I could remember—two to three times a day, in fact. I would tiptoe to the bathroom scale as the needle would groan to 200, 205, 210, and up and up. In tears and disgust, I would stumble off the scale, angry that all my efforts at counting calories, reading diet books, eating expensive, packaged diet foods, watching infomercials, and buying the guaranteed-to-help-you-lose-weight-equipment had failed me again. I looked in the mirror, and guess what? I was still FAT!

Sally's Experiment in Three Parts

Dr. Jantz said he'd like me to conduct a thirty-day experiment. I said I was open to almost anything at this point, but what he suggested seemed so bizarre that I almost laughed. First, he asked me to bring my scale to our next session. My scale? My trusty security blanket? A thousand times NO, I said to myself. But a week later, I brought it in, feeling very foolish as I muscled it into the office in a large, plain, brown paper bag. I felt as if I were a kind of felon waiting to be caught for smuggling contraband. I was told my scale had gone on vacation and that I could have it back anytime I wanted it. I thought this was fairly strange therapy, but I promised to go along with it. Then, Dr. Jantz asked me to make an agreement with him that I would do three things on a regular basis. Here is what he asked me to do:

1. The first thing I was to do was to start eating a simple, healthy breakfast each morning. That was my only guideline, that it had to be healthy. No list of special foods, no restrictive diet, no number of calories to count, lie about, or eat. Nothing. Just "Sally, I want you to eat a healthy breakfast every day." What surprised me was that I was told to make my *own* decision and not rely on someone else's idea of what I should eat. I was given complete freedom to eat when I wanted and how much I wanted. It just had to be healthy. Frankly, this frightened me, because I wanted to be told what to do.

Here's what I did. I chose to eat a large breakfast of whole-grain cereal and low-fat milk and some fruit each morning. It was bulky so it made me feel full. It wasn't sugary, so my insulin level did not increase. I knew all about this theoretically, but it wasn't easy to put into practice. A big part of me (which was most of me) hated it. I missed my ordinary morning fare of two jelly donuts and three cups of coffee with lots of cream, followed in a few minutes by grazing in the fridge for a few leftovers from the night before. But I'd made an agreement, and besides, I was desperate.

2. The second thing I was asked to do was even more amazing. I was not to weigh myself at *all* between sessions. I'd already sent my scale "on vacation," so there was no way to weigh myself at home. But I was not to weigh myself *anywhere*. Not at the home of a friend, not on a public scale, not downtown where they sell scales, *nowhere*. This was difficult. How was I to know if I was making any progress if I couldn't weigh myself two or three times a day as I'd done most of my life? I didn't understand it, but I said I'd be a good person and obey the rules.

3. The third thing I said I'd do was something I had not done in years. *Exercise*. After I had received a complete medical evaluation, everything was set to go. But still, when you're over two hundred pounds and gaining fast, the last thing on earth you want to do is exercise. Lifting a finger to help a friend was too much work for me. I certainly wasn't going to be seen in a health club with those trim, young things doing aerobics as if they were made out of willows. But Dr. Jantz told me my activity would require no money, no club membership fees, no time, no expensive equipment, and no detailed book of instructions. Here was my assignment: to engage in an enjoyable activity each day, to choose whatever I wanted and do it for as long as I liked, but to move my body and have fun. What was this weight-loss professional talking about? I asked myself. How was I going to lose weight permanently unless it was 1) hard work, 2) no fun, 3) expensive, and 4) something that would take all my time and embarrass me in the process?

Sally's Awakening

It's almost with tears I tell you this, because at this point I got in touch with something deep inside. For the first time in memory, I was making my own decisions about my life—small as those decisions were—eating a healthy breakfast, not weighing myself, and choosing my own activity. I started to feel good about myself. *Hey, Sally, you're not so bad after all. Yes, you're still fat, but something's happening to you that's never happened before. You're taking control of your life in a new way. Maybe this is the answer you've been searching for in vain for so long.* I remember wiping the tears from my eyes as I sat down at my kitchen table to write down the various kinds of activities I could do that I enjoyed. The list turned out to be pretty short. I decided to walk fifteen minutes a day. I'd worn a well-beaten path to the refrigerator over time, but I had not taken an intentional walk in the great outdoors for more than ten years. *Sally, you did it! You made a decision all on your own. No books told you what to do, no infomercials, no calorie-counting gurus—you did it all by yourself.*

I lived only three blocks from Puget Sound in the state of Washington, but could not remember the last time I had walked on our beach. Now there I was, walking fifteen minutes a day, enjoying the scenery, smelling the crisp air of the beautiful Northwest I'd not smelled in years, watching great eagles fly overhead, and losing weight permanently? That was the hard-to-believe part. What did all this have to do with joining the two percent? But I kept walking day after day. I enjoyed my walking so much that one morning I discovered I'd actually walked for thirty minutes. Overweight Sally? Walking thirty minutes? But it was true. My stress was going down; I was finding myself relaxed, more content, happier. In fact, on some very good days, I didn't even think about losing weight. I simply trusted what I was doing. I was enjoying my own company once again.

A New Kind of Treatment

I would go to see Dr. Jantz once a week. It was a great experience for me because I'd talk about how relaxed I was starting to feel, how I wasn't yelling at the kids as much, and even though I still had challenges with my marriage I had begun to enjoy a greater sense of well-being. The funny thing was that we seldom talked about food. A weight-loss professional not talking about food? It was uncanny. But I was still thinking about food constantly. I confessed that thinking about food occupied 110 percent of my time. I still wanted to think that food was my problem, and I was ready to blame it for just about everything.

But in spite of my misguided thinking, after four weeks I realized I was starting to lose weight. Unbelievable. I had decreased my "grazing" on food by nearly fifty percent and had become much less compulsive in my eating. I was no longer using a scale at all. (It's still in Dr. Jantz's office along with a dozen others, I think.) I now realized for the first time what a judgmental device a scale actually is; always telling me whether I'm good or bad, up or down, this way or that. I was no longer into *good* or *bad*. My focus now was to take control of my life. I had given diets too much power, scales too much power, other people's opinions of me too much power, calorie-counting too much power. Now, I was moving toward progress with less and less thought of perfection.

To make a long story short, after two years I have shed over eighty-five pounds, and I've never felt or looked better in my life. I eat only healthy foods, drink lots of water, exercise regularly, and no longer blame anyone for anything—not even past abuse or my unhappy childhood. It has not always been easy. To be honest it's *never* been easy, and there have been times when I've binged on food for as long as three days at a time. But with professional help and a determination to join those who lose weight permanently, I'm confident that I'm now on my way, and so you can be on *your* way. I wish the same exciting, healthy results for you.

Not an Exception

Sally is just one of many who are losing weight permanently. I still see her, but not as often. Recently, she showed me a picture of how she looked when we first got together, and there is almost no resemblance to her former self. Sally's journey toward permanent weight loss started with a simple thirty-day experiment, one I would encourage you to begin today:

1. Eat a healthy breakfast every day.
2. Put your scale away and quit weighing yourself.
3. Find an activity that makes your body move, and do it every day. You choose the activity, when, and how long to do it.

Take the *high dive* experiment of re-establishing yourself as executive director of your life. It will take some time to readjust, but knowing beforehand that you are bound to go through difficult—but painfully positive—emotional withdrawal and physiological cravings will help you understand the process. Remember, you are interested only in progress, not perfection. Like Sally, you, too, are entering basic training—a tough but vitally necessary boot camp for people who choose to lose weight permanently.

The Water Factor

Sally learned that eating too much didn't make her fat, but rather eating the wrong kinds of foods made her put on the pounds. She already knew that calories played _some_ kind of role in weight loss, but it was not the role she thought it was. As we worked together to help her develop her own nutritional program, she began to understand that simply cutting down on the amount of calories would never contribute to long-term weight control. The important question was _calories from what kinds of foods?_ She also discovered that until she faced things in her life such as anger, hurt, and the emotional abuse she'd experienced as a young girl, she would never join the two percent. She was amazed at how intricately she was put together—emotionally, spiritually, physically, and psychologically. She knew that if she didn't take a serious look at her _total self_, she would never achieve the results she wanted so desperately. One of the most critical things she learned immediately—and the easiest to change—was the importance of drinking lots of water.

The Joys of H_2O
Water helps curb your appetite by helping you feel full.
DRINK WATER!
Water helps you maintain critical muscle tone.
When you drink lots of water, you do your skin a huge favor.
DRINK WATER.
Water keeps you regular. When your body gets sufficient water, the colon functions better and you are a lot happier!
DRINK WATER
(P.S. Eight glasses a day keep the fat away.)

Sally learned that water was essential to her life and health, so she started drinking a couple of glasses each day. Then it increased to three, four, and now six or more glasses of water every day. One day Sally called me and said, "Dr. Jantz, I'm drinking lots of water, but I'm also beginning to feel aches and pains I haven't felt for years. What's going on in my body? I think I'm drinking too much water." Many people have what we call a "healing crisis" as the body goes through a major transformation. As we get healthier, sometimes old symptoms flare up (that we've buried for years by simple denial of our problem) only to be treated through improper eating and bingeing. I told Sally it was normal to feel some of those aches and pains, and therefore not to be overly concerned unless they persisted. Within a short period, she had moved away from that discomfort and eventually forgot she had gone through it at all.

I'm convinced that Sally will be a water drinker forever. To make it more convenient for her to enjoy water at home, at work, or in the car, she now simply fills one-liter bottles from a water purification system she had installed at her kitchen sink. You'll hardly ever see Sally these days without her water bottle. She's hooked, and what a great drink to get hooked on.

Anyone can start a healthy nutritional program *by drinking lots of water.* Begin by drinking one or two glasses with each meal. You will feel fuller faster, and it will not do your body any harm. (Of course, if you have severe problems with indigestion or other health concerns, you should check with a health professional to make sure this water-drinking regimen is right for you.) If it's difficult for you to drink lots of water, you may want to mix in some squeezed lemon or low-sugar fruit juice. The more water you drink, the less you will want to consume caffeinated soft drinks, diet colas, and beverages high in sodium. In fact, before long, all those sodas you once drank so casually will taste so sweet you'll hardly be able to get them down. When that happens, pat yourself on the back, because you've begun to make great progress.

What We've Learned from Mice

Once Sally began to enjoy the physical and emotional benefits of water, we then worked together to help her develop a plan to improve the rate at which she lost weight by eating not less food, but the right foods. We talked about the many experiments scientists did with mice who were put on the "supermarket" diet: cookies, butter, ice cream, sugary foods, peanut butter, processed foods such as salami and baloney, white bread, cheeses—all those high-fat foods that taste so good but also guarantee maximum weight gain.

Here's the interesting thing about the experiment with the mice. Each mouse received carefully controlled portions of the "supermarket" diet—not large amounts. In other words, the mice were not allowed to binge! During no time in the experiment did they overeat. Still, they got enormously fat because they ate consistent amounts of the *wrong kinds of food*. If they had eaten the same amounts of the right kinds of food, they would have remained healthy and slender.

This study was a revelation to Sally. She immediately saw the connection with her own eating habits. Even though she knew a lot about diets and nutrition, she had always held the view that she would have to starve herself to become thin. However, by simply changing the kinds of foods she ate— along with drinking abundant amounts of water, doing sensible exercises, and promising not to weigh herself—the pounds began to drop, and they continue to disappear.

Five Keys to Joining the Two Percent

There are five basic components of a healthy diet:

One . . . Limit the fat! People who lose weight permanently learn the benefits of decreasing the amount of fat in their diets. Sally was among that group of Americans who consume forty percent or more of their calories from fat. That's too much fat. When Sally started understanding the reports of the increased risk of heart disease and cancer associated with these high levels of fat, she immediately corrected herself. She started reading labels in the supermarket and began to understand the wealth of information they contained. This was a far cry from the ineffective calorie counting and roller-coaster dieting of the past. She was now getting the kind of information she could use to keep her on track. She stopped frying her foods and quit breading meats. She learned that broiling, baking, and even microwave preparation were better alternatives than cooking foods in fats and oil.

She also started eating more lightly steamed vegetables. Her former overweight self had also eaten vegetables, but they were "doctored" foods such as creamed corn, fried onion rings, and carrots swimming in deep pools of rich butter sauce. She learned that the difference between one plain baked potato and a baked potato with "the works"—mounds of butter and gobs of sour cream—was enormous, and that she'd have to eat at least *nine* plain baked potatoes to equal *one* with all the good stuff that's really so bad.

Two . . . Limit refined carbs! Counsel for cravers:

1. Look in your cupboards, desk drawers, and glove compartment and remove all unhealthy snack foods.

2. Substitute sugarless gum for these high-fat snacks. People who lose weight permanently learn to limit the amount of refined carbohydrates in their diet. Sally grew up with an overweight mother who loved to prepare big, fattening sack lunches for her daughter to eat at school. The sandwiches were works of art, prepared on soft slices of white bread, overflowing with greasy salami, baloney, and thick layers of mayonnaise and butter. Nestled in the bottom of the bag would be a love note, accompanied by two or three homemade chocolate or peanut butter cookies. Her mother may have had the best

of intentions for Sally, but those good wishes later brought on disaster for a little girl now grown up and struggling with her weight. Unwittingly, Sally's mother had played into the hands of food manufacturers who are consummate professionals when it comes to catering to our nation's taste buds. They know we want sweet, not bland; tasty, not necessarily healthy. But people who lose weight permanently ignore the hype, the ads, and the promotions because they know it will make them fat and keep them fat forever.

Three . . . Limit the sodas! People who lose weight permanently say good-bye to artificially sweetened drinks. We don't need those sodas, diet colas, or caffeinated beverages. They do nothing but increase our insulin level and keep us dependent on still more sweets, making it impossible for us to give up our addiction and move toward healthy foods. Water, water, water . . . is the only alternative worth drinking.

I hate my FAT enough to:
- Do something about it right now, not wait until after the holidays to become part of the two percent who lose weight permanently.
- Throw out the bags of snack foods I've hidden in the cupboard even though I paid good money to buy them.
- Eat an apple or orange before I go to the movies so I'm not tempted to buy all the junk at the food counter.
- Begin treating myself as a person created in God's image, and therefore believe I am someone definitely worth caring for.

Signed _____

Date _____

Four . . . Eat complex carbs! People who lose weight permanently eat large amounts of lightly steamed or raw vegetables, fresh fruits, and whole grains. This was a stretch for Sally at first, because she and her family had never eaten this way. But over time, Sally, her husband, and their two children started to see the health benefits of this new way of eating. Today, they no longer sit down to watch television with large bags of corn chips, potato chips, or other empty-calorie snack foods nestled in their laps. For them, it was a major step toward successful weight loss. Not only do these products contribute to the expanding midsection of the average American, but they are actually becoming a national health risk. American families may be getting most of their refined carbohydrates during the so-called down times when they snack and graze for food, usually when they are bored or watching television.

Sally already knew her body turned carbohydrates into sugar and that when she ate fast-food items her sugar level would rise. She'd feel a burst of energy for a couple of hours, only to dip later to zero. She'd been there all her life. Dramatic highs, and equally dramatic lows—causing her to feel tired and listless. So what would she do to try to regain her strength? Get up and eat more of the same junk food. Remember, our definition of insanity is to do the same thing over and over and expect a different result.

Today, it's different in Sally's household. She and her family snack on raw fruits filled with all-natural sugar and fresh, raw vegetables without the fattening sauces and dips. While her children still like to go out for an occasional hamburger at fast-food restaurants, Sally makes sure there is a salad bar for her.

Complex carbohydrates have virtually no processed ingredients. Chemically, complex carbohydrates are composed of the kinds of sugars that break down much more slowly in your digestive system. This means they are absorbed more evenly into your bloodstream, keeping your insulin level steady. As you increase the amount of complex carbohydrates in your daily eating, you and your family will feel better because of the change.

Five . . . Listen to your body! People who lose weight permanently learn to pay attention to their body's appetite signals and eat when they're hungry. This was perhaps the most challenging—and frightening—thing Sally had to learn. Sally became overweight over time because she ate more than her body was able to get rid of. Because she often ate when she was not hungry, or *didn't eat* when she was, she was never able to lose weight. Chronic dieters such as Sally are completely out of touch with the biological mechanism that controls their weight. They feel they must starve to lose pounds. Wrong! A person who keeps herself hungry long enough will eventually begin bingeing on foods that will send the blood sugar to the moon. And this pattern will create more hunger as those foods are absorbed, and then still more cravings for the same kinds of food. The result is a vicious cycle of hunger and bingeing. It takes the place of normal eating and drives a person even further away from what she wants most: permanent weight loss.

The Original Meaning of Food

Dieting and bingeing were tremendous obstacles to Sally's physical health and mental stability. Each round of dieting caused increased hypertension and a rise in her blood pressure. When she started to believe in her heart that dieting and bingeing were making her more prone to stress-related illnesses, heart ailments, kidney disease, and stroke, she knew she had to make a change. To do this, Sally had to start listening to her body. She had actually forgotten what it was like to eat normally. In the past, she had engaged in so much secret eating, bingeing, squirreling away money for snacks, lying about finances, and hoarding of food, that Sally no longer knew what it was like simply to eat food *to provide nourishment and strength for her body,* and not to medicate a self-induced condition called overeating. That's why Sally had to learn the art of eating regularly again—three times a day. She now eats a healthy breakfast of light carbohydrates, usually composed of a whole grain cereal with low-fat milk. It's bulky so it makes Sally feel full. It's also not sugary, so she never feels a rapid rise in her insulin level. Sally's breakfasts now satisfy her until noon, when she can then eat a good lunch without having even to think about bingeing.

If Sally had not chosen to change her views on nutrition, she would have remained fat permanently. That was not an option she chose to live with. She knew there was no middle ground. Healthy and slim; unhealthy and fat. That same choice Sally made is also yours. Sally says,

> When I quit dieting, I began to lose weight. When I started drinking water, I started to lose weight. When I quit drinking three to four diet drinks a day, I started to lose weight. Without anticipating it, my clothes began to feel looser, more comfortable. I began to enjoy my walks on the beach. I also began to eat nutritional supplements—not diet pills—that were specially designed for people like me who are in recovery from binge eating. The good news is that during the past two years, I lost over eighty-five pounds, and I'm proud to say I'm going to keep it off for the rest of my life.

You've Got to Go through It to Get to It

What Sally didn't tell you is something you need to know. As people allow their bodies to go through the necessary physiological transformations during weight loss, they also may experience a wide range of emotional transitions. For every ten pounds Sally lost, she would look in the mirror to see what she was becoming—and liked what she saw. But Sally was not alone in seeing her body's transformation. Other people—including men at work—also started noticing her. They gave her positive comments and paid attention to her as never before. This was uncomfortable for Sally, and on more than one occasion she became so frightened that she reverted to food as her friend and confidant. But with help, and a goal of weight loss always before her, Sally learned to self-correct. She'd come so far in her struggle, had begun to feel so good about herself, and was so sure she was on the right track, that she chose to deal with all the issues that might otherwise have defeated her.

Be Kind to Yourself

Certain basic measures can help people deal with the types of emotional stress created by the changes—good changes—that come about as one loses weight.

- Give yourself time. It took you a while to put on weight, and it will take time to make it go away.
- Get your body moving, but do it gently and easily. Exercise will do wonders for your body and for your emotional state.
- Don't let the popular culture decide what you should look like. You make the decision and then stick with the nutritional plan that works best for you.
- Being thin does not guarantee happiness, and being over your ideal weight does not mean you will have a poor self-image. The question is, what do YOU want for YOU?

One day an innocent comment from a male coworker really threw Sally. "You look terrific . . . better than ever. It's great to see you looking so great!" Because of the struggle Sally was having with her husband at the time, it felt good to hear someone say something so nice about her. She loved the positive male approval. But it also scared her. *What do I do with this approval? Did I make a mistake in losing all this weight? Have I opened my own Pandora's box?* These were questions Sally never needed to ask before because she had always masked her sexuality with fat. We talked at length about her fears, and I reminded her that they were natural concerns in the context of her emotional growth. Sally chose to use the stuff of her daily life to work through her fears, learning that she could now trust herself. She could even begin to accept—and enjoy—male attention without allowing it to become a sexual issue.

Sally realized when she discovered food freedom that she regained a God-given personal power that allowed her to grow spiritually. Once shunted to the outer reaches of her life, God now became vibrant and alive to Sally. Once socially unaware and purposely inattentive to the needs of others, Sally now searched out those who needed a friend and started developing healthy relationships. Sally's story says it all, because she represents one of the two percent who lose weight permanently—emotionally healthy people who keep growing at all levels of their lives.

Because Sally chose a healthy, whole-person approach to weight loss, she was now able to think about other areas of her life—in some cases for the first time in years. Earlier, her entire focus had been on food: what to eat, where to eat, and how to avoid dealing with life by eating. Now, food was simply a nutritious fuel to give her the needed strength to become the person a loving God had created her to be. With her new-found freedom also came a renewed sense of responsibility. It gave her permission to become executive director of her life. No more blame, and no more shame. For Sally—and also for you—food freedom means the ability to create and maintain a healthy relationship with all the intricate parts that make up you—the spiritual, physical, relational, emotional, and relational you. Sally now had more time to do things she had not done for years. She had always enjoyed music and has now become accomplished on the violin. She started reading again—not just diet books. She discovered, as you will, that when one works on the development of the whole person, food will assume its natural role. That's because those who lose weight permanently feel less compulsive about life and therefore are able to explore and nurture exciting, new dimensions of their lives.

One of Sally's Assignments

After I'd seen Sally for a few months, I asked her to increase her activity level by another ten percent, which she did. I also asked her to begin spending fifteen minutes a day journaling, talking on paper about the three deadly emotions of anger, fear, and guilt. She would write about anger, for example, under such headings as ongoing frustrations, rage, resentment, and bitterness. She examined all the different shades of anger that came from her past or were still troubling her in the present. Then, after fifteen minutes, she would close her journal, no longer worrying if her grammar was perfect, if she'd dotted all her *i*s, or crossed all her *t*s. None of that mattered anymore. She was learning that even in her writing her goal was progress, not perfection. She knew she was on her way to wholeness and health the day she looked into a mirror and said, *You know, Sally, I look at you in this mirror today, and I really like what I see. You really are becoming the person your loving heavenly Father meant you to be. Finally, your big, loving heart is expressing itself again, no longer hidden by fat. You are on your way. Because I love what you are becoming, I will never medicate you with food again.*

As time went by, Sally just kept jumping off what we called the high dive, dealing with the deep issues of her life such as hurt, blame, fear, anger, and guilt. It's not been easy, but nothing is easy that is truly worth pursuing. She keeps taking her walks, longer and longer excursions now, is increasing her exercise activity, can be seen drinking lots of water, and is an inveterate label reader. She pays close attention to her nutritional plan, has eliminated foods that are not healthy, and has become a *dynamic* instead of a *desperate* human being. Just ask any one of her many friends. She has allowed her big, loving heart to come forth and express the unique person she truly is. Sally knows that permanent weight loss is an inside job.[2]

Action Plan #6

Design a Nutrition Plan that Works for You

1. Do what Sally did.

   a. Eat a healthy breakfast every day and eliminate fat from your diet.

   b. Engage in an activity you enjoy for fifteen minutes each day. The only rule is to *move your body.*

   c. Put your scale away.

   d. Start drinking water *and eliminate all sodas and diet drinks.* Do all this for thirty days, then weigh yourself.

2. Begin a confidential journal that describes your innermost feelings. In your journal or notebook, take a daily

inventory about how you feel about the three deadly emotions that must be dealt with by people who lose weight permanently: anger, fear, and guilt. You are not writing an essay for anyone else. *These are your own personal expressions.* Write on these areas for one month.

3. Begin using the proper dietary supplements *(not* diet pills) to help you nourish your body, which may have been too long deprived of proper nutrients. Choose supplements from a source that you trust. It's important that these supplements are designed specifically for people *in recovery.* If you would like more information on the availability of such products, please call The Center for Counseling & Health Resources, Inc. at the number given in the back of this book. If you are under the care of a physician for a particular medical condition, check with him or her before beginning the supplements.

4. Examine your emotional health. Studies indicate that eighty percent of people with eating disorders have been a victim of some form of abuse. If you experienced abuse, it may have been verbal, sexual, emotional, or physical. Write down your thoughts on your past. How have past events pushed you toward food? Based on what you've read in this chapter, how can you best deal with that past and join those who lose weight permanently? If your abuse was long-term or extreme, we strongly suggest you make an appointment with a professional counselor.

5. Read and listen. Fortunately, there are some great books and audios now available to help you get on track to permanent weight loss through healthy, balanced nutrition. These are not diet materials, nor are

they intended to foster guilt or create shame. Here are six products I highly recommend:

Eat Smart, Think Smart by Robert Haas (HarperCollins). Haas is a world-renowned nutrition expert who presents a breakthrough program for maximum mental and physical performance.

The Psychology of Living Lean by Denis Waitley, Ph.D. (USANA). In this new twelve-cassette audio series, Waitley has brought his many years of experience in behavioral studies together and has produced one of the best, most balanced programs for a healthy lifestyle on the market today. This series is fully compatible with Dr. Jantz's approach to permanent weight loss and represents a breakthrough audio program.

Graham Kerr's Kitchen by the "Galloping Gourmet" Graham Kerr (Putnam). In his inimitable style, Kerr makes the kitchen a wonderful place for creativity, discovery, caring, learning, and sharing. A great book to help you with healthy, balanced cooking. A *must* for every kitchen and every cook.

Thin Tastes Better by Stephen P. Gullo (Carol Southern Books). Gullo's contribution to the weight-loss field comes in helping the overweight person to identify and conquer *trigger foods* that subvert, to change our "food talk," and to weigh ourselves with a "new scale," to mention only a few of the reasons Gullo remains such a qualified spokesperson on the subject of weight control.

Dr. Cookie Cookbook by Marvin A. Wayne, M.D., and Stephen R. Yarnall, M.D. (Quill). This is a great, fun-filled book to help you "dessert" your way to health with more than 150 delicious *low-fat* cookies, cakes, and treats. A gold mine of healthy information for you and your family.

Wellness Medicine by Robert A. Anderson, M.D. (American Health Press). Most people ignore their health until it is lost. *Wellness Medicine* offers the most comprehensive book to date for implementing life-style changes needed for optimal wellness. Dr. Anderson is the clinic physician for The Center for Counseling & Health Resources, Inc.

In case this chapter has made you hungry, and I hope it has *for the right kinds of foods,* let me leave you with five practical nutritional tips:

1. *If you crave something sweet* after dinner, enjoy a fat-free yogurt. You'll feel better than if you had a piece of pie, a dish of ice cream, or some other sinfully delicious dessert.
2. *A European supper* consists of bread and soup. Try this two to three times a week for dinner. That's your main course, not a warm-up to the entree. Make it a broth or vegetable-based soup to keep it low in calories and fat. *Bon appetit.*
3. *If you want to order a rich dessert* at a restaurant, split it with someone else at the table. It's automatic weight control.
4. *If you're invited to a party,* enjoy one or two pieces of fruit before you go *so you are not hungry when you arrive.* Be full enough so that if the caterer does not appear you will not be disappointed—or famished!
5. *Eliminate oils and fats when cooking.* Nonfat yogurt is a good substitute for sour cream, and chicken broth

for your sauces is a sneaky—yet healthy—disguise for butter.

Now you are ready to explore the exciting possibilities of establishing and maintaining a greater closeness with your family, colleagues, business associates, and friends—the user-friendly subject of chapter 7.

Notes
1. Sources: Snack Food Association; U.S. Department of Agriculture.

2. Some of the nutritional information in this chapter has been summarized from the audio series *The Neuropsychology of Weight Control, Tape #7* (SyberVision Systems, Newark, Calif.).

7

People who lose weight permanently know the value of

DEVELOPING INTIMACY WITH PEOPLE

Kindness in words creates confidence. Kindness in thinking creates depth. Kindness in giving creates love, and kindness towards oneself—body and soul—provides the atmosphere for a lifetime of love and appreciation.

Gregory Jantz

The U.S. Environmental Protection Agency is charged with controlling the use and disposal of toxic chemicals. The EPA decides, for example, whether a new form of toxic substance, such as a pesticide, may be registered for consumer use. If it is considered likely to cause inordinate environmental damage or to be carcinogenic, the EPA can refuse to allow the product to be brought to the marketplace—in the interest of public safety. However, even with increased EPA regulation of such toxic substances, new pesticides and hundreds of other new compounds are marketed each year. Many are not intended to enter the environment, though through waste and accidents they eventually do.

What, you may ask, is the above paragraph doing in a book about people who lose weight permanently? Why are we suddenly talking about the EPA, environmental damage, and toxins that cause damage to life and limb? In one way, it has nothing to do with the subject at hand. In yet another way, however, it has much to do with the topic of this chapter. People who have severe weight challenges are also loaded with life- and people-threatening *emotional* toxins of many varieties—not necessarily carcinogenic, but just as destructive to "relational tissues." These toxins keep spouses, colleagues, and relatives at bay, reduce a person's chances for success, and keep that person stuck on a course of permanent weight gain.

In 1976, Congress passed the Toxic Substances Control Act, which required the EPA to be informed of the estimated production, volume, uses, and health-related studies for every new commercial chemical. If evidence exists that a substance may cause cancer, create genetic changes, birth defects, or death, it is then designated a "substantial risk" and can be regulated or banned.

What if we were to band together to pass an equally powerful *Personal Toxic Substances Control Act,* a watchdog agency to inform the public of the relationally toxic substances that keep us fearful, out-of-control, unkind, uncaring, inattentive to others, overweight, and generally discontent with our lives? People who lose weight permanently learn the importance of removing from their lives toxins that have subverted their growth and kept them from becoming the men and women God created them to be. As these toxins are flushed from their systems, they begin to learn the importance of intimacy—that closeness to others that has eluded them for so long. The relationship with the spouse deepens and becomes meaningful. They find themselves at home in social situations where they were never comfortable before. They learn to risk. They learn to forgive, and they spend more time building bridges of friendship than destroying them. Is this what overweight people wanted when they began their whole-person approach to losing weight permanently? No, it wasn't.

Virtually every person who comes to The Center for weight counseling simply wants to lose weight. What each one discovers, however, is that he or she is wonderfully and beautifully made, so intricate, in fact, that the challenge of weight loss simply becomes a byproduct of becoming a growing, giving, loving person who knows how to be close to others and no longer afraid. This is what true intimacy is all about.

> Searching for oneself within is as futile as peeling an onion to find the core: when you finish, there is nothing left but peelings; paradoxically, the only way to find oneself is to go outward to a genuine meeting with another.—*S. Harris*

It takes time to develop this kind of intimacy, because for people with weight problems, intimacy has usually been the farthest thing from their minds. For many, it takes a long time even to *want* to develop and expand this part of their big, loving hearts. And it is often very painful. So painful, in fact, that some wonder if it's worth the struggle. Perhaps that's how you feel at this point. But the two percent who lose weight permanently will tell you that learning the true meaning of intimacy is worth the struggle, the risk, and the pain.

A Shift from Food to People

Why, then, a chapter on relationships and intimacy? Because growing, healthy people work on active reconciliation. They create and maintain positive, healthy relationships. They are never satisfied with the *status quo*. Once intimate with food, people who lose weight permanently have made the shift to getting close to people and establishing deep, long-lasting friendships they never thought possible.

The Child or the Manuscript

The story is told of a passenger on the Titanic who was an author with a manuscript on which he'd worked for many years. Confident it was a great piece of work, he was preparing it for publication. He plunged into the sea on that fateful night in mid-April, 1912. As the British passenger liner sank in the North Atlantic, he held on to the one precious thing in his life: his manuscript. Then he saw a child in the water. He could not cling to the manuscript and save the child. What should he do? He released his precious work to the dark waters and swam to the child. The child was dead. He found another child, alive, held her up, tried to get into a lifeboat, but it was full. He grasped a nail on the side of the lifeboat. It pierced his hand, and there he hung by that nail. The manuscript was lost, but his soul was found. What the author did that night was more noteworthy than if his manuscript had become a bestseller.

Just like the author who thought he could not live without his precious words, we, too, often think we cannot live without the ingrained patterns of our past—whether they be good or bad, positive or negative. But people who lose weight permanently know that if they are to grow in every area of their lives they must look at every area of their lives. This is what forty-three year-old Kathy had to

> **The biggest disease today is not leprosy or cancer. It is the feeling of being uncared for, unwanted—of being deserted and alone.**
>
> **Mother Theresa**

learn to do, although when she first came to our clinic, it was not on her list of priorities.

Kathy's Story

Kathy grew up in a family where she was never allowed to feel much of anything. So it was no surprise that early in childhood she found an effective way to hide her feelings. She learned to become a people-pleaser. If her parents wanted her to be perfect, then she would become perfect by neither thinking nor feeling. Emotionally, Kathy ceased to exist. When I asked her to talk to me about her life, it was as if the cat suddenly had her tongue. She sat there in bewildered silence. "I really can't say. I just don't know." Kathy had been married for twenty-three years, and from outward appearances her family seemed happy: involved in church, community life, and the PTA. But as she slowly began to open up, she confessed that she'd always felt disconnected from everyone, never able to bridge the gap, never close to her husband, and even distant from her children. There was a constant, terrible emptiness that kept knocking away inside, a void that started early in Kathy's childhood.

With a noncommunicative father who expected her to be the perfect child, Kathy was given a huge burden to bear. She never had the privilege of sharing what little courage she had with the one who was responsible for bringing her into the world. She never remembered getting a hug from her father, not even on her birthday, or at Christmas, or when she was baptized at the age of ten. Now, grossly overweight at age forty-three, she looked back at that rejection with adult eyes, fearful of opening what she said might be a Pandora's box of pain she'd be unable to deal with. Yes, she wanted to lose weight, "but what does my father and my background have to do with it?" she asked.

When I asked Kathy to talk to me about her current intimate relationships, she froze, unable to speak or move. She sat there as if in shock. I suggested that perhaps she had numbed the last four decades of pain with food, and that she may not really have any intimate friendships—that she had coped the best she could. But she was not a defective human being because she'd responded in this way.

As I spoke, she raised her bowed head slowly, and with tears flowing said that it was probably all true. She had been a lost soul for most of her life, simply hoping that it would one day get better. For Kathy, the word intimacy had too narrow a definition. She thought of it as only the physical act of sex, which never had been satisfying. It was no surprise that her sexual side was also disconnected, devoid of desire and light years from intimacy.

> "She had discovered a miracle drug to numb her pain, and no doctor's prescription was required. It all seemed so safe. As long as she continued to mask her inner anguish with mounds of food and the layers of fat they produced, she would never find out who she was or become the person God intended her to be."

When I shared with Kathy that intimacy meant feeling close to someone, her immediate response was, "I can't do that." Yet she'd been intimate for years with food rather than people. This was her way of getting her unmet emotional needs met. Kathy desperately needed to be loved and nurtured, but it never happened. Once the coping pattern had been established early in life, it was relatively easy for her to continue to use food as a coping mechanism when she reached adulthood. Even in her coping, she'd been a "good" girl. She hadn't gone the route of alcohol, drugs, promiscuity, or other forms of rebellion. Food was her friend, her confidant. She did her best to keep most of her compulsive behavior in the socially acceptable categories: watching television, obsessively cleaning house, drinking diet colas—as many as six to eight cans a day and secretly hiding the empty cans because it was getting so expensive and increasingly difficult to hide.

She occasionally joined a small group Bible study, but she would last for only two or three sessions, and she was gone. *Getting close to people was too frightening.* She moved her family from the small fellowship they'd attended for years to a larger one where she felt she could hide more effectively. If Kathy did attend an intimate social event at church or in the community, her tension would build to such intensity that she would go home and binge on food. Food—lots of food in a short period of time—was the only thing that gave her joy. Food was her clandestine lover and her friend. She had discovered a miracle drug to numb her pain, and no doctor's prescription was required. It all seemed so safe. As long as she continued to mask her inner anguish with mounds of food and the layers of fat they produced, she would never find out who she was or become the person God intended her to be.

People who substitute intimacy with food for intimacy with others share certain characteristics that make them prone to this behavior.

Characteristics of Families of Those with Food-Related Problems (See also appendices 1 and 2.)

1. Perfectionistic
   - high expectations from father, either verbal or nonverbal
   - often first-born
2. Mother frequently dieted
   - over-emphasis on weight and appearance

- compulsive dieting, fasting
- diarrhetic use
- laxative abuse

3. Father distant
   - intense desire to please father
   - father unavailable emotionally

4. Parent (often mother) codependent
   - mother denied own needs
   - mother assumed responsibility for everyone else

5. Rigid discipline with severe punishment
   - guilt and shame used to motivate
   - rules communicated, "It's not okay to be a child"
   - humiliating or hurtful punishment

6. Sexuality ignored or considered "dirty"
   - children not given basic information
   - no opportunity to discuss sexual issues

7. Daughters used as confidantes
   - father complained to daughter about mother
   - child used as parent's primary form of emotional support

8. Children forced to be adults
   - daughters who "raised" other siblings
   - children not allowed to be children themselves

9. Children victimized in *any way*
   - fondling
   - incest
   - neglect
   - verbal abuse

10. Parent (often father) addicted
    - prescription drugs
    - alcohol
    - street drugs

11. Family members tend to ignore or deny negative emotions
    - explosive anger common

- anger and sadness never spoken of
- negative emotions covered up by behaviors aimed at pleasing others
12. Overuse of food for pleasure or reward
    - food the primary focus for pleasure
    - emphasis placed on sweets and rich desserts

It's unfortunate that Kathy was able to relate to many of the issues presented in the above chart—from perfectionism, to a distant father, to a mother hooked on diets, to an intense desire to hide her own feelings by pleasing others. In addition, she was unable to deal with troubling issues during puberty when boys made fun of her body, her height, her complexion, and her large breasts. The humiliation was more than she could handle. But the more she hid her emotions, the larger she became. By the time she left high school, Kathy weighed 180 pounds. In my book *Healing the Scars of Emotional Abuse,* I describe the emotional pain of unresolved anger and resentment. Such anger stems from:

- the sense that you've been treated unfairly

- the belief that no matter how hard you tried, it never made any difference

- the fear that it was really your fault they treated you that way

- the realization you were misguided to believe that someday your parents would change

Kathy eventually expressed some of these feelings as she emerged from a learned helplessness to what she called a tiny flicker of hope. She was no longer willing to use the inner space of her heart to store garbage from the past. She knew

> "She was no longer willing to use the inner space of her heart to store garbage from the past."

God had given her a higher purpose for living. Sadly, there are millions of ten-year-old Kathys in our country right now who are getting a raw deal. That's why the two percent who lose weight permanently are willing to do whatever is necessary to help turn the tide for themselves and everyone they meet.

Compounded Addictions

Few addictions—food included—stay solo for long. Addictions are like fly paper. They attract other addictions, other erratic or compulsive behaviors. When they are compulsive in nature, we call these co-addictions. Kathy's main co-addiction was watching television for hours at a time, particularly the daily soap operas that provided her with a fantasy life to help get her through the pain of her real existence. In fact, she crossed the line of fantasy, actually putting herself into certain character roles so forcefully that she lived her life around the TV soap opera schedule. She would not answer the phone or the doorbell during the broadcast, even if it were a friend or neighbor. If she had to miss a program, she'd set the VCR on record and watch the tape later that night. She devoured the soap summary magazines and kept stacks of past issues next to her ten years of unread *National Geographics* stored in the garage. While television was a secondary addiction—as strong an example of intimacy with an inanimate object as you could imagine—she kept her first addiction with food going full strength. And then she added a further addiction: spending.

Her husband would say, "Dear, I gave you a $20 bill yesterday, but you have cash receipts from the ATM totaling $100. You're sure taking a lot of money out, aren't you?"

"Well, you know, honey, I had to buy an expensive present for Johnny's friend's birthday ($5 actually spent), and then I had to get a full tank of gas (actually only spent $6.25), and then I paid cash for an expensive dress for Susan ($9.50 actually spent at a discount store). The costs really added up."

Look at your own life. Are you afflicted with any of these obsessive/compulsive co-addictions?

- Gambling

- Television viewing

- Secret spending

- Sugar cravings

- Secret smoking

- Pornography

- Lying—"white lies" addiction

Kathy simply lied with half-truths. Yes, she bought some things. But they didn't cost as much as she implied. In fact, she bought cheap items totaling around $20. The rest of the ATM money went for junk food that she quickly squirreled away under the bed, in the attic, in the garage, and even in the trunk of her car. While there was always a grain of truth in response to her husband's inquiries about money, Kathy's response was always couched in a bigger, bolder lie.

Going Off Automatic Pilot

For your ongoing emotional growth and your permanent weight loss, it is important that you look at whether you have avoided—and may still be avoiding—intimacy on some level. Intimacy issues have interfered in your life and sabotaged your success at weight loss. Now is the time to say, "I need help." There's no point in blaming your past, your family, or even a former abuser, if any. You have simply had numerous unmet needs that you attempted to address through intimacy with food. Now you are moving away from such erroneous thinking and are moving toward the two percent who lose weight permanently.

For Kathy it was necessary to engage in several *high dive* experiences—painfully effective behaviors—that challenged past beliefs with positive encounters. We began our high dives wherever there was fear, hurt, misunderstanding, or frustration. Once Kathy convinced herself that her problem was not about weight, she became open to some suggestions.

Six High Dive Principles to Build Intimacy in Relationships

One: Face your challenges head-on. If you choose not to, your compulsive behaviors will remain. Overeating, secretive spending, an obsession with television, hiding food, lying, and whatever behaviors you may be engaging in seem innocent enough. In fact, they are a chain on your body and a tether to your soul, dragging you to places you do not wish to go. Become aware of what is happening to you, in you, and around you.

Two: Put yourself in the company of a variety of people, difficult though it may be. It could be a small Bible study, a support or therapy group, a community project, fellowship group, the choice is yours. But choose something to join now. There's a saying that *you can't get to second base with one foot on first.* It's the same with the challenge you face in moving closer to others. Move quietly away from your past isolation and get involved at the most basic level with other people. Even if you do not participate fully in the event, at least have the courage to be present. You can't learn to swim by reading a book, and you will never achieve intimacy with others unless you take the risk of being in their presence.

Three: Discover what kinds of people are a challenge to you. What types of individuals trouble you or seem to make you feel uncomfortable, self-conscious, or ill-at-ease? Who are these people in your life? Are they neighbors, relatives, a boss? If you are a woman and are uncomfortable around men, put yourself in the presence of trustworthy men with whom you can practice being the kind of person you are becoming without losing your personal power or your identity. Let's say you are threatened by men who are especially good-looking. If that is the case, make a conscious attempt to attend a social gathering at church, at the office, or in the community where attractive men will be present. You don't even have to talk to them. Just be *in* the social setting as a relaxed, comfortable woman who deserves to be there without being intimidated.

Four: Survey your past. Look at those relationships that have involved conflict, hurt, and pain, and therefore need to be resolved. You may have been the receiver of the hurt, or you may have been the giver. Whichever, look at the conflict squarely and determine to do something redemptive. People who lose weight permanently learn to do this on a regular basis. They see and feel the hurt, and they forgive. He may have hurt you in the meanest way, and you may want him to suffer even more than you. "Nothing is bad enough for that man!" Such an attitude is understandable, but not acceptable if you are committed to emotional growth.

You may ask, "Am I supposed to forgive my father for the years of sexual abuse, the emotional neglect, and all the other hellish things he did to me?" Yes, that is what I'm saying. If you would be whole, you must take the chance of forgiveness, the risk of being made a fool of, of not being understood, of swallowing your pride, because there is simply no other way to become the whole person you want to be. Begin to empty the storage tank of emotional toxins and past resentments that are making you sick and keeping you fat. Do you remember when Peter asked Jesus, "Lord, how often will my brother sin against me, and I forgive him? Up to seven times?" Jesus answered, "I tell you not up to seven times, but up to seventy times seven." The point was not to forgive 490 times, but to forgive, and forgive, and forgive, and then to keep on forgiving. That was the wisdom of two thousand years ago and it has not changed.

Five: Select two or three people and work on improving your relationship(s) with them. These might be people you work with, live with, or come in close contact with on a regular basis. Write down three ways you would like to see your relationship with them improve. Then begin to work on enriching that relationship. Because you have been a food addict, you may have assembled a group of codependents who have not been honest with you about what was going on in your life. Now is your opportunity to take the offensive and begin to effect positive changes in your relationships. Be aware that your former compulsive eating has made an impact on others. Choose a few people with whom you want more honest, healthier relationships. Then begin to use the principles in this book to help bring your objectives into reality.

Six: Look for creative ways to solve your interpersonal problems. Emotionally healthy people are problem-solvers and bridge-builders in relationships. They understand that we were never made to go it alone. No one is an island. Deep within each person with a weight problem is a big, loving heart that desperately wants to touch someone, hug someone, love someone, and be touched and loved in return. You may be off the scale when it comes to anger. But please never forget: the damage is not permanent. You are becoming free to be authentic again. You need no longer allow your addictions, unresolved anger, or compulsions to hide your big, loving heart.

The following nine suggestions will help you move into new, creative, and effective relationships with others:

1. *Do something to "let off steam" without hurting someone.* You might try hitting your pillow, doing some physical exercise like running, or taking a few very deep breaths and counting to ten.
2. *Try to laugh at little irritations instead of letting them get to you.*
3. *Find out what really made you mad.* Look beneath the surface for the root problem.
4. *Write an angry letter* to the person or situation that got you upset. Be totally honest about your feelings, and then tear up the letter.
5. *Express your anger at God* if you feel angry at him, but then allow him to speak to you.
6. *Confront the person you're mad at—but only after you've calmed down, and do so gently without blaming or getting emotional.*
7. *Learn to forgive others and yourself.*
8. *Direct your anger in constructive ways.* For example, if it makes you mad that so many people in our world are hungry, volunteer to work at a soup kitchen on weekends.
9. If you find that you consistently can't handle your anger in appropriate ways, *get help from a professional* counselor.[1]

The Quintessential Meaning of Intimacy

In one of the most moving books I've ever read, entitled *Letters to an Unborn Child*, David Ireland, disabled, confined to a wheelchair and terminally ill, wrote a series of letters to the unborn child he would never meet. While his wife was expecting, Ireland took the time to write letters to be read one day by his unknown son or daughter. Here is an excerpt from one of those letters. It takes the word *intimacy*, elevates it to sky-splitting heights, and defines it as I've never heard it described before.

> Your mother is very special. Few men know what it's like to receive appreciation for taking their wives out to dinner when it entails what it does for us. It means she has to dress me, shave me, brush my teeth, comb my hair; wheel me out of the house and down the steps, open the garage and put me in the car, take the pedals off the chair, stand me up, sit me in the seat of the car, twist me around so that I'm comfortable, fold the wheelchair, put it in the car, go around to the other side of the car, start it up, back it out, get out of the car, pull the garage door down, get back into the car, and drive off to the restaurant. And then, it starts all over again: she gets out of the car, unfolds the wheelchair, opens the door, spins me around, stands me up, seats me in the wheelchair, pushes the pedals out, closes and locks the car, wheels me into the restaurant, then takes the pedals off the wheelchair so I won't be uncomfortable. We sit down to have dinner, and she feeds me throughout the entire meal. And when it's over she pays the bill, pushes the wheelchair out to the car again, and reverses the same routine.

And when it's over—finished—with real warmth she'll say, "Honey, thank you for taking me out to dinner." I never quite know what to answer.

Every week, sometimes twice a week, I have to wash my hair; this involves sitting with my shirt off in front of a sink. There's a mirror there and I am able to look at myself, which otherwise I rarely can. Each time I see my concave chest, my head leaning to the right—the muscles and flesh of my arms and shoulders having slowly disappeared over the past few years—I begin to feel depressed, and Joyce will say, "Oh, don't look! I'm going to take that silly mirror down if you don't stop admiring yourself."

Then perhaps a little later I may be lying on the bed taking a nap, and your mother will sit down next to me. She'll place my hand in her lap and, looking into my eyes, with all depth of sincerity she will say, "You're so handsome to me. You're the most handsome man in the world. I love you so much." And somehow, out of the ancient well of our experience together, I know she means it.[2]

Intimacy is what we all ultimately desire, whether we admit it or not, whether defined as the white heat of romantic passion, the caring for a colleague, the depth of a friendship, or, as experienced by David Ireland, the uncompromising love and compassion of a woman who knew her husband would soon die and leave her alone to raise the precious child he would never see.

Joy unspeakable comes to you when you open your heart to see, touch, and feel the goodness of others, to experience your own depth, and to make it your business today—and every day—to nourish your spirit even as you shower those around you with love and compassion. People who lose weight permanently know what it means to draw closer to others—to develop an intimacy that one writer has called *into-me-see*. That's it. That's the secret: the willingness to let others see the real you—the big, generous, loving heart you hold inside.

Kindness in words creates confidence. Kindness in thinking creates depth. Kindness in giving creates love, and kindness towards oneself—body and soul—provides the atmosphere for a lifetime of love and appreciation.

Action Plan #7

Questions to Help You Get Closer to Others

1. Ask yourself: What emotional toxins have been building up inside me that have driven me to become intimate with food? Whom have I not forgiven for past hurts? Be specific.

2. Which people do you continue to allow to hurt you emotionally? Why? What specific adjustments are you willing to make to stop allowing this to happen?

3. Based on what you have learned in this chapter, how does forgiveness relate to intimacy? Read Psalm 139; Matthew 6:7-14; and John 8:34-36. How do these verses help you let go of past resentments and move ahead to your happier, brighter future?

4. Based on where you are right now, with what three people can you develop a closer relationship? What will you do with each person to help create the first steps toward intimacy—coming closer together—during the next three months?

Daphne Rose Kingma writes in her daily guide *A Garland of Love,*

Nothing will make you happier or make you feel more like yourself than the true, disclosing, emotional exchange of yourself with another human being. Nothing is more wonderful than being able to tell someone else who you are, to open your heart, to reveal your true colors, to engage with another person at the level of your own refinement.

Today, step across whatever shyness or fears you may have, and allow yourself with someone you trust to make the small—or immense—disclosure that for a long time you have wanted to make. What an incredible joy it will be to be present as yourself.[3]

Perhaps this chapter on intimacy has provided you with the kind of hope, promise, and joy that will help make losing weight permanently worth the painful joy it will become. Your new adventure starts the moment you allow yourself to love the person you are inside—that good person with the great, compassionate, overflowing heart—even as you recognize there will still be great challenges as you keep growing toward emotional health, something we talk about in chapter 8.

Notes

1. Chris Lutes, "What to Do When You're Angry," *Campus Life,* January 1991, p. 54.

2. David Ireland, *Letters to an Unborn Child* (New York: Harper & Row, 1974), p. 33.

3. Daphne Rose Kingma, *A Garland of Love* (Berkeley: Conari Press, 1992), entry for February 26.

8

People who lose weight permanently recognize

EATING PROBLEMS AND THEIR LINK TO ABUSE

Time cures sorrows and squabbles because we all change, and are no longer the same person. Neither the offender nor the offended is the same.

Blaise Pascal

A brilliant woman pianist once gave an intimate performance for a group of society woman in the sun-drenched library of a country estate. Later, while dessert was being served, a guest approached the pianist, gushing, "I would give anything in the world to play as you play."

The virtuoso looked at the woman for a moment and said, "I'm sorry, madam, but I don't think you would."

Red-faced, but undaunted, the guest tried again, quietly this time, "But really, I truly would give anything to play the piano with the skill that you do."

The pianist, realizing she had not successfully made her point, said, "No, my dear, I'm afraid you really wouldn't. If you would, you might play better than I, at least equally as well. Yes, you'd give anything *except your time, the one thing it takes to be good.* You wouldn't sit on a bench practicing hour after hour, day after day while your friends were out

151

having fun, enjoying parties such as this and otherwise getting on with their lives."

Then she smiled. "I hope you understand that I'm not criticizing you. I don't even know you. I'm just telling you when you say you'd give anything to play the piano as I do, that in your heart of hearts you don't really mean it. You really don't mean it at all."

> You gain strength, courage and confidence by every experience in which you really stop to look fear in the face. You must do the thing you cannot do.
> Eleanor Roosevelt

That story is about one very honest woman. The talented pianist knew that in music only a few succeed at what they attempt, even though most will say they *want* to be great, famous, well paid, and acknowledged with their name ablaze in lights. But in reality, only the dedicated few will realize that dream. Likewise, among those who try to lose weight permanently, only a few succeed. But with practice, discipline, and dedication, those few can include you.

You Are Not Alone

One of the primary ways you will do this is by consciously disconnecting food and its associations from all forms of abuse that may have occurred in your life. As you read this, you may say, "I've never been abused sexually, physically, or emotionally, so this chapter has nothing to say to me." You may be right, or you may be engaging in some form of denial. That is for you to discover as we go along. Or you may say, "There really may be something to this idea that past experiences keep me going to food for comfort, and I'm willing to take a long look at my past to check out the connection." Or you may say, "I *know* that my eating problems are intricately connected to the deep hurts of my past. I am finally willing to engage in the battle *where it actually exists:* in my mind."

No matter how you respond to the message of this chapter—and I am aware that it may be difficult to read—you need to know you are not alone in your struggle. At times you may feel as if your picture would be next to the definition of loneliness in the dictionary, but not only do you have friends like me who are on your side; you also have a loving heavenly Father. You may have thought you were doing a solo performance as you engaged in your silent, compulsive behaviors, but guess what? You were not alone then and you are not alone now. Even more important, you are no longer addressing the symptoms of your problem as you've done in the past. You are now choosing to deal with the issues that really matter.

> An approaching storm can be either amazingly beautiful or terrifyingly frightening. It all depends on one's attitude toward storms.

Have You Ever Been Told . . .

People who have problems with food have related food to past unresolved events—most of which have been painful and abusive—or at least past events that you've never quite dealt with or put to rest. In the last chapter you became more aware of the need to strengthen your relationships. You are now in a great place—perhaps the best place you've ever been. But there is still a lot of work to do—especially in dealing with your past pain and how it may still be driving you to engage in certain behaviors today.

Begin by answering these questions:

- Have you ever been told you were a bad boy or girl?

- Have you ever been told you were stupid, or that you'd never amount to anything, no matter how hard you tried?

- Have you ever been told your sister was prettier than you? that your brother was smarter? that your classmates did better work than you?

- Have you ever been told you were lazy . . . and God help you if you turn out to be like your father, or mother, or uncle, or aunt?

Do any of these questions fit? If so, you have been affected by "faulty past programming," which is a form of emotional abuse. As a child, if someone said you were ugly, or dumb, or not as smart as someone else, your brain believed it—even if you knew it was not true. Left unresolved, those thoughts may have festered, become deeply ingrained, and eventually become so much a part of you that they ruled your life.

Perhaps you're like Susan, who told me, "When I get angry, I start overeating. That's just what I do. I can't help it. Being angry makes me want to clean out the fridge, and binge till the cows come home." There are a couple of ways to address this issue. One, we can try to change what makes Susan angry (which may be difficult, since the source of her anger may be many years old, and the person or persons involved may not be around to change). Or, we can try to help Susan change her response to the anger. This is a key point. Just as Susan *learned* to overeat when angry, so can she *learn* to replace patterns with new, positive behaviors. It all starts with self-awareness. Not to replace positive behavior for past negative programming is to live a life that is forever out of control, careening emotionally from wall to wall, and living with knee-jerk reactions.

Three Messages

I want you to write down three strong messages you received in early life from a parent, other family member, church member, peer, or teacher that you now feel suggested that you were not all right as a person. Then jot down the effects of this on your life. What behaviors have they elicited from you? How have those comments, made so long ago, made you feel about yourself *in today's world?*

My Past Messages

1. _____
   _____
   _____
   _____.

2. _____
   _____
   _____
   _____.

3. _____
   _____
   _____
   _____.

Please use more paper or your journal to expand on your answers. This is your opportunity to express yourself as fully and confidentially as you wish.

Now I want you to address the following twenty questions that will help you see if you may have connected any of your current behaviors to past programming. If your answer is yes to the question, place a check mark in front of the question. If it is no, write nothing.

___ 1. Did your family engage in the kinds of activities that you presently use to overcome bad feelings?

___ 2. Did your family engage in behaviors similar to yours to celebrate good times?

___ 3. Did any of your siblings ever engage in addictive or compulsive behaviors?

___ 4. Have any of your close friends engaged in such behaviors?

___ 5. Have people close to you ever told you they were concerned about your behaviors?

___ 6. Do you compare yourself to others of the same sex for size or other physical characteristics?

___ 7. Are you afraid of attention from the opposite sex?

___ 8. Would any of your behaviors be considered a "sin" or a serious wrongdoing by your religious affiliation?

___ 9. Do you turn to food to relieve your stress?

___ 10. Do you tend to feel inadequate at your job, at school, or in your home?

___ 11. Is your weight beyond what would be considered normal for your body size and type?

___ 12. Do you struggle to try to maintain a regular exercise program?

___ 13. If you exercise, do you do it compulsively?

___ 14. Do you feel guilty about how you spend money?

___ 15. Do you tend to feel that others are better than you?

___ 16. Do you feel guilty about things in general?

___ 17. Do you feel as if God is distant from you? unapproachable?

___ 18. Do you feel isolated from people and terrified by closeness?

156

__ 19. Do you avoid church or severely limit your appearances at social gatherings?

__ 20. Do questions like these make you feel uncomfortable?

If you checked five or more questions on this survey, I urge you to reflect on the questions and see what past messages may have influenced your behavior.

**Remember, you are not what you think you are.
But what you think, you are.**

The past is the past. It may have been hurtful, abusive, and unfair. But those events no longer need to trigger your desire for food. That's why it's important for you to deal with the idea that something is defective about you, that you're just not good enough, and that because you engage in compulsive behaviors you are hopeless. This is simply not true. You are not defective. You were, however, an unwilling participant in bad programming. The shame heaped on you by persons in your past says more about them than it does about you. You no longer need to live a life of paralyzing fear that propels you toward food as your safe haven and intimate friend.

People who want to lose weight and keep it off know they have the option of two sets of characteristics on which they can build their lives. You, too, have these options. One is a litany of destructive traits, behaviors that give you a wild, built-on-sand, ineffective, out-of-control, guilt-laden, emotionally draining life that wears you out, tears you up, and leaves you an emotional skeleton. When you choose these traits, you live out your negative past programming in an equally negative, unsatisfying present. Your other option is a series of constructive traits which provide for boundaries, forgiveness, a belief in what is positive, and a deep respect for yourself and others. Here is an expanded list of both sets of traits. As you read them, ask yourself, *Which of the two am I prepared to live with for the rest of my life?*

TWO FORMS OF EMOTIONAL LIFE

Destructive Characteristics

- Frantic living
- Extremes
- Addictions
- Insecurity
- Lack of consistency
- Fears of abandonment
- Low self-esteem
- Loneliness
- Frequent and unexplained physical ailments
- Discomfort
- Fighting for control
- Excessive guilt
- Lack of personal freedom
- Deception, lying, hidden agendas
- Taking sides and power plays
- Spoiling through meeting material instead of emotional needs
- Rules without meaning
- Religious addictions
- Boundary issues
- Lack of fun/enjoyment
- Making comparisons
- Punishment (shame-based) instead of discipline
- Unrealistic expectations

Constructive Characteristics

- Respect for individual differences and personalities
- Consistency in word and deed
- Sense of security and comfort
- Problem-solving based on mutual concern and under-standing
- Belief in positive outcomes
- Acceptance in disagreements
- Understanding of possible repercussions
- Clear boundaries with everyone, including family members
- Self-confidence
- Freedom to develop and express one's own gifts
- Ability to give and receive opinions
- Ablility to forgive
- Moving beyond the past as a reference point for the future

Jennifer also had a choice between these two sets of traits. But it was not until she was well into adult life that she realized she had better options than the ones with which she grew up.

Jennifer's Story

Jennifer's parents divorced when she was ten. For years she tried to gain the approval of her birth father, whose communication was confusing and unclear. He fought unfairly and made promises he did not keep. From Jennifer's standpoint, he possessed many of the nonenduring traits on the previous list. Jennifer had no reason to live her life with confidence. Those closest to her had let her down, drained her emotionally, kept her self-esteem at a low ebb, and punished her with shame. Of course, all parents make these kinds of mistakes, but for Jennifer they were particularly destructive because of the number of them and the way that Jennifer took her parents' mistakes to heart.

With unresolved pain and unrealistic expectations guiding her young life, Jennifer turned to sex, drugs, and bingeing on food as her way of coping with anger and disappointment. When she was in her late twenties, she was still living out the pain of the negative messages of the past, choosing not to deal with the emotional abuse that had clouded her early life. When she married at age thirty-one, her life was so out of control that by her own admission she wondered if she would survive the first year of marriage. That's when she sought help. Here are Jennifer's own words:

When I was a teenager, I figured I knew what I was doing. I was rebellious, angry, and would hurt anyone I could—especially my parents and stepfather. My life was so out of control that I didn't know up from down. My lifestyle almost killed me. I don't know how I even made it to age thirty. I was so lonely, so afraid, so grossly fat, and completely without hope. But then, someone said there was a place of hope where they helped people like me. So I decided to get help for my weight problem. I was surprised to learn that food and overeating were not my problems at all—I just thought they were.

I had to learn to reprogram my life from its negative past to a more positive, hopeful present and future. But we hardly ever talked about food or my weight. Instead, the counseling was always something like: "Jennifer, have you become a more grateful person? Jennifer, how are you doing in the forgiveness department? Jennifer, you seem to have a deeper respect for yourself and others. Good for you. Jennifer, isn't it great that you can take some time and grieve about your past, but then close the book on it, and open it again to a fresh, new chapter called the present—one you can now share with your new husband, and eventually your children?"

I was looking for help in losing weight. But what I really lost was my unconscious reliance on years of programming that were still making my life a hell on earth. I am now at peace—still a bit heavy—but that is not the issue. It never was. Jennifer has been transformed. I have learned to become my own parent, providing myself with new values that are guiding my life. And if I can make these changes, believe me, *anyone can*—anyone, that is, who's serious about getting his or her life together.

No Shame, No Blame

The good news is that you, too, can learn to re-parent yourself, just as Jennifer has done. In fact, the truly mature person becomes his or her own mother and father. Think about the impact of that statement. This means *you* get to set the rules. *You* get to do the disciplining. *You* get to do it all. You can still have respect for your parents or caregivers, but you no longer allow them to be executive director of your life. If you have been programmed for helplessness and hopelessness, now—as your own parent—you have the privilege of programming yourself for joy, love, acceptance, kindness, and peace.

Now you can quit blaming others for your problems. Your parents didn't *make* you an overeater. They may have helped create an environment out of which you chose an addiction to food, but they did not make your choices for you. In fact, they were also victimized by circumstances and people. But people who lose weight permanently don't even know how to *spell* the word blame anymore. They do not blame their parents, their grandparents, their DNA, their personality, their church, their abusers—if any—or other negative influences from their past. They simply recognize that what happened, happened, and now is the time to get unstuck.

> Objects of great worth are taken care of, protected, and prized. It is time to stop thinking of yourself as of no value. If you are having trouble finding your value, look to friends, caring family members, and God.

Let's take a look at some of the abuse you may have suffered in the past, or that you may be suffering right now. Here's a key thought: All trauma causes us to seek relief. The question is how will you seek that relief? People do things for one of two reasons: because they *relieve tension* or *achieve goals*. If you release tension through food because it feels good, is easy to do, and demands no thought on your part, then that decision will make you fatter, unhappier, and more prone to blame others for your problems. If, however, you live your life with a sense of seeking goals, then you shift your focus to a brighter, more confident future. That's why this prayer is so wonderful:

Lord, what you give me the awareness to perceive,
and the strength to believe, I trust you to help me achieve.

Someone once asked trumpeter and entertainer Louis Armstrong to define jazz. He responded by laughing and saying that if you've got to define it, you just don't get it. We could say the same thing about abuse. If it's happened to you, you don't need to define it. But let's look at the ways that obsessive/compulsive behaviors may be linked to abuse.

How Current Symptoms May Be Linked to the Past

1. A person may feel a constant undercurrent of anxiety or depression. This person is fearing the reoccurrence of a past abusive event. This may also result in mood swings, irritability, and sleep problems. Someone who was hurt by her father may develop a fear of men and in adult life may invent coping mechanisms that prevent intimacy with the opposite sex.
2. Present-day events may remind someone of past trauma and thereby produce emotional distress.
3. People who have suffered abuse may feel confused or have difficulty concentrating.
4. Flashbacks are painful events. When people experience flashbacks of traumatic events they may use unhealthy means—such as bingeing—to numb the pain and prevent recurrence of the flashbacks. These people may also experience a large number of nightmares.
5. People who have suffered abuse often have difficulty with intimacy. The people with whom they were intimate as children—their families or other trusted adults—abused them, so trust is now very difficult. This results in a sense of detachment and estrangement from others (the *into-me-see* of intimacy).

We are not attempting to dredge up or create false memories. This book is not about witch-hunts, nor is it a psychological board game called *Blame the Past*. You need to look at and acknowledge that what you remember could be inaccurate, and that it is normal to have incomplete memories, particularly of the first seven years of life. Later memories of childhood may be blurred or fragmented also.

Try to determine the difference between what really happened and what may have been a childhood appraisal of an event. For most compulsive overeaters, there was some form of deep trauma. But there are also Interpretations of events that may make more innocent occurrences seem traumatic.

Your thinking is different now from what it was during childhood. You may have confused emotions with fact. As a child, the difference between your imagination and reality was blurred. That's why we don't want to suggest abuse that wasn't present, but we do want to say that whatever happened *did* affect you. In some cases it was clear what happened—such as the woman who remembered and recorded each graphic detail of being sexually abused for ten years. Her experience was more than a bad dream. It was a nightmare that happened.

It's helpful to try to determine the difference between what really happened and what may have been a childhood appraisal of an event. However, keep in mind that for most compulsive overeaters there *was* some form of deep trauma. We know this to be true from years of counseling.

Up until now, you may have questioned your sanity, asking, *What's happening to me? Am I losing it? Why can't I cope with life?* Wouldn't it be exciting to discover that you were simply responding automatically to past programming, and that now you no longer need to do that? Now you are free. You've learned the truth about yourself, and it has liberated you forever. Try the following exercise.

A Family Interview

Imagine that your parents are very old and do not have long to live. (Do this even if they are deceased.) They are making a surprise visit, coming to ask your forgiveness for the many inappropriate ways they may have treated you. Write out in detail what they might say to you. Write with deep feeling, touching those areas that have hurt you most. Here are five positive things that may happen to you during this exercise:

1. You can give yourself permission to resume the position of executive director of your life.
2. You can learn to forgive your parents—whether they are alive or dead.
3. You can free yourself from the bondage of past hurts because *you* are finally writing the forgiveness script.
4. You can release the poisons and toxins of the past and replace them with the power and strength of your new-found freedom.
5. You can become aware that you no longer need to carry the burdens of the past, because you are free at last.

Understanding Generational Patterns

You will soon discover some amazing things just by looking with adult eyes at your past. Take some time and write your answers to the following questions. Use a journal or notebook, as these questions may take several sentences to answer.

1. What do you think were your mom's and dad's areas of greatest challenge as parents? How did their areas of weakness affect your family's daily life?

2. Do you remember certain ways of relating that characterized your family—perhaps the youngest was always treated like a baby, or perhaps everyone was always positive about the future? How did your family's pattern affect you? Are you still living out those patterns? If so, how? Are the patterns healthy or unhealthy for you?

3. Write about your mother. Who was she? What were her strengths and weaknesses? Often people's strengths are also their weaknesses—e.g., a mother who had a strong work ethic may have neglected her family at times when there were many tasks to be done.

4. What was your mother's situation like? For example, was she caring for a dying relative while trying to raise children? Was she dealing with a divorce or financial hardship while you were being raised? Did she have health problems or was she going through menopause during your adolescence? Viewing your parents as real people who had their own emotional needs and difficult circumstances can help you understand them, though it does not excuse abuse.

5. During adolescence and early adulthood, was it easy to grow up and separate from your mother? Is your current relationship one of mutual respect and independence? If not, what factors may have contributed to the difficulty to separate? Are you still trying to please your mother? In what ways?

6. If your relationship with your mother is strained, is there guilt involved? Who makes whom feel guilty? If you are the one feeling guilty, how do you handle it? Do you ever respond with compulsive behavior?

7. Were you told you were pretty or handsome as a child? If not, what do you think you were told? Sometimes when parents try to be helpful ("If you let the hem down on that dress it will cover up your knees") they

communicate lack of acceptance *(she thinks I have ugly knees)*.

8. How did people in your family communicate? Was there open and honest communication or were things hidden? Were you able to express your opinions, or did you feel you had to hide them?

9. Now think about your father. What was he like during your childhood? What were his strengths and weaknesses?

10. What were your father's circumstances? Did he have physical or health problems that affected him while you were growing up? Did he have to deal with difficult conditions at work? Was he ever unemployed for long periods of time? Did he seem happy with his work or chronically upset with it?

11. How did your father make you feel about your body? Did he affirm you as a growing girl or boy? In what ways? If not, how did he talk about your body or your growing up?

12. What expectations do you think your father had for you? Were you able to fulfill them? If not, did you think he was disappointed in you? Did you ever check that out?

13. What are three important sayings or three values that were strongly taught in your home? Have they been guiding lights for you or blinding lights?

14. What spiritual values, if any, were taught in your home? Were these consistently taught and followed, or was there inconsistency? Was your parents' religion judgmental or freeing? Did it teach love or self-hatred?

For the overeater, unpleasant or incongruent childhood experiences are often the triggers that continue to drive them to food for solace and comfort as adults. For example, if your mother was highly critical of you, your weight, and the ice cream you ate, then as an adult you may continue to go to ice cream in anger. In fact, you may be so hooked into this past experience that even something as innocent as a phone conversation with your mother may trigger your urge to run to the fridge and eat a half gallon of ice cream. That is the power of an unresolved past.

As we talk about the past, you may be recalling events that are triggering complex emotions and old ways of acting. If so, I urge you to talk to a counselor who will understand you as a whole person and will help you now.

No family is perfect. But the damage our families do, either intentionally or by accident, is not irreparable. Since you are learning to be your own parent, you have the privilege of repairing yourself. You can do it now because you are an adult. You *couldn't* do it as a child. But you have changed. Hope is now within your grasp. You no longer need to punish yourself with destructive behavior. You are free to become the person God created you to be.

Denial Is a River in Egypt

You no longer need to deny your past. You have the courage to face what happened early in your life, recognize that's *not* who or what you are today, and press on. The denial of the past has served its purpose, even though it was ineffective, which was to keep your damaged self-esteem in check and to prevent it from being overwhelmed. But continuing to deny your past would result in the following:

1. If you choose to avoid confrontation with your past, your compulsive behavior will probably become more extreme.
2. If you do not talk about your pain, your compulsive behavior will probably worsen. You can't change something

you refuse to talk about. Keeping past pain a secret prohibits you from letting your own unique identity emerge and keeps you from being authentic. People who are successful with their weight loss talk, and talk, and talk to counselors and friends, and out of that counseling and conversation eventually comes healing.

3. If you do not deal honestly with your past, you will remain an emotional toxic dump. If you do not review and attempt to understand your past, how can you seek and give forgiveness? How will you learn to deal with conflict? How will you understand the basics of healthy communication?

You know in your heart that *if it is to be, it's up to me*. Congratulations on your progress thus far. You are well on your way to joining those brave, gutsy, no-more-nonsense, two percent who lose weight permanently.

Action Plan #8

A Cause for Celebration

1. Write out five ways in which you are different—in a positive way—from your parents or those who raised you. Be as specific as possible.

   a. _____
   b. _____
   c. _____
   d. _____
   e. _____

2. Write a letter of freedom to your parents, but do not give it to them unless you are working together with a counselor. Acknowledge that they did what they

169

could—most parents do their best—and much of it was good. However, there were also issues that were hurtful to you. Acknowledge this in a spirit of love. Talk about your newfound freedom from the negative events of the past and how they no longer are allowed to be the fuel for your food addictions. Write how you have been liberated to become your own parent and are now ready to perform all that that role demands.

3. Read the letter you wrote in #2 to a trusted friend. Then go to a safe place, such as a beach, picnic grounds, or the edge of a lake, and burn the letter. In front of your friend and witness say, "I'm now letting go of my past, and will no longer allow past hurt or abuse to direct my life. I am finally free to become the person God created me to be."

4. After you've completed this action plan, give yourself a non-food reward, such as going to a movie or a play, or taking a long walk on the beach, or sharing some of your new insights with a friend. Whatever you do, take action, and do it in a spirit of joy and celebration.

I close this chapter with nine principles to help you move to the next rung in your growth to become the emotionally healthy person you desire to be as you join those hearty souls who lose weight permanently.

NINE STEPS TO GREATER EMOTIONAL HEALTH

➤ **Step 1**
Admit you need help.
Make the shift from "I can do all" to "I need all the help I can get."

➤ Step 2
Develop unconditional love.

Learn to respect yourself and others, regardless of what you or they do.

➤ Step 3
Learn to be accepting.

Learn to disapprove of past and present inappropriate behavior, but not reject the behaver.

➤ Step 4
Work at self-discipline.

Let go of the past. Do not let it cloud your present or future. This will help you keep long-range objectives in focus.

➤ Step 5
Resolve past conflicts.

Your freedom to join the 2 percent is connected to how effectively you deal with past hurts.

➤ Step 6
Learn to listen.

When others speak, they may be giving you the answers you have been looking for.

➤ Step 7
Learn to share yourself.

Share your joys and your sorrows with those who have ears to hear. The feedback you receive will be part of your growth.

➤ Step 8
Change your attitudes.

Accept all obstacles and challenges as valuable learning experiences. It's still true: *no rain, no rainbows*.

➤ **Step 9**

Learn to forgive.

There is little possibility for you to change without demonstrating a spirit of forgiveness.

In this chapter we've focused on how past hurts may have been instrumental in pushing you toward food as medicine, friend, and all-round comfort. Now let's turn to how you can maintain your new life and new weight even through the difficult times.

9

People who lose weight permanently know they can

MAINTAIN MEMBERSHIP IN THE TWO PERCENT CLUB

Listen to this wise advice; follow it closely, for it will do you good, and you can pass it on to others: Trust in the Lord.
Proverbs 22:17-18, TLB

As I was looking for an appropriate opening to the last chapter of this book, I hoped I would find a story filled with spiritual truths, psychological insights, and motivational thoughts. After a diligent search I happened across a torn piece of paper I'd once used as a bookmark. I remembered that it was during a particularly difficult part of my life that I'd copied these words down on a scrap of paper. They are the simple lyrics to a well-known Shaker hymn that, in a few sentences, sums up what we've been talking about for eight chapters. It is a message for all times, an encouraging word for you about simplicity, freedom, humility, and *being in a place that's right*.

'Tis the gift to be simple
'Tis the gift to be free,
'Tis the gift to come down
Where we ought to be;
And when we find ourselves

In the place just right
'Twill be in the valley of love and delight.

When true simplicity is gain'd
To bow and to bend we shan't be asham'd,
To turn, turn
Will be our delight,
'Till by turning, turning
We come 'round right.

Simplicity. Getting the clutter out of your life and focusing on the really important issues like faith, hope, love. Finding the place that's right for you, far from the madding array of past guilts, fears, obsessions, and compulsions. Not being afraid to bend your head in humility, recognizing that you wear no shroud of shame when you face your past, but that, in fact, only by turning, turning, and turning again will you make the corrections you must make to *come 'round right*. This is what this book is all about. It is my prayer that it is also what *you* are all about.

> I will no longer hold myself to perfectionist standards. I will be satisfied with what I do, knowing I can always make changes that will be in my best interest. From now on, I will accept all compliments from others with a heart of gratitude.

Someone has said we humans have a tendency to crucify ourselves between two thieves: the regret of yesterday, and the fear of tomorrow. They rob us of precious years of productive labor and love. We cannot change our past, only accept it. Yet the regrets and the "if only"s keep us from living in the present and looking to a better future with excitement and joy. So how will you stay the course? How will you remain part of the two percent who lose weight permanently? Let's look at some proven, creative ways to help you meet your objectives.

Seven Disciplines to Help You Stay the Course

1. **Let discipline start at home.** A man prayed fervently, "Lord, fill me, please fill me." A friend standing nearby said, "Don't bother, Lord, he leaks." When there is little or no discipline at the center of your life, you leak. If you wish to lose weight permanently, you will not allow the many distractions of life to throw you off course. Discipline your desires and be willing to postpone gratification for the sake of a better future. Be too large for worry, too hopeful for despair, too kind to hurt another, and too committed to ever give up.

2. **Discipline your priorities.** Just as sometimes there is a difference between a person's character and reputation, so there is sometimes a chasm between what one says and what one does. Your success depends on being consistent. Emulate the priorities of the two percent who lose weight permanently, and you will stay the course.

> **From this day forward, I will be optimistic about my progress—regardless of its pace. I will put worry on the shelf and will refuse to give in to despair.**

3. **Discipline your nerve.** Whenever you choose not to face the reality of your life and its challenges, you weaken your character. General Omar Bradley said,

"Bravery is the capacity to perform properly even when scared half to death." Is the whole-person approach to permanent weight loss frightening? Yes, for some. Don't forsake permanent weight loss for lack of courage to do what's right.

4. **Discipline your follow-through.** There are few sports where the follow-through is not vital, and it's particularly true in activities such as tennis, baseball, and golf. Why do ninety-eight percent of dieters fail to keep weight off permanently? They don't follow through.

5. **Discipline your time.** Have you ever said, "I don't have time." If so, what you really meant was, "I have not yet made it a priority." People who lose weight permanently know that it takes time to lose it and keep it off. The process cannot be rushed. They learn what is important is not necessarily urgent, and what is urgent is seldom important. That's why we have mentioned over and over that this is a journey of progress, not perfection.

While cleaning out his desk one day, a man found a three-year-old shoe repair ticket in the back of a drawer. He realized *that's* where his favorite pair of shoes had been. He went to the repair shop with the ticket, and to his surprise, the repairman said the shoes were there. "May I have them now?" he asked. The man replied, "I'm sorry, sir, they're not quite ready. Could you come back Friday?" The man *had* enough time. So do you.

6. **Discipline yourself to "what is."** Check out reality. Like a moth attracted to a light, you may be batting your wings at something that will never get you anywhere, as bright and exciting as it may appear. "If I were only younger, or thinner, or smarter, or richer, or lived in a different neighborhood, or had a better background . . ." These are the words of one who lives in a world of fantasy. You will begin to achieve success

when you know where the battle lines are drawn, and then fight on those lines.

In the Old Testament, we are told that the people of Israel had to live on something called *manna* while traveling through the desert on their way to the Promised Land. This was their daily diet for forty years of wandering. It appeared with the morning dew, and the Hebrews were instructed to gather only what was needed for one day, because any surplus would spoil. Why did they call it *manna?* Because

> **Gentleness with yourself is neither arrogance nor dishonesty. It is taking the reality of your life and treating it with the respect you deserve.**

they didn't know what it was. The word *manna* means "what is it?" It was reality. And they got it one day at a time. For you, your *manna* is what is staring you in the face right now. It's your loves, fears, challenges, joys, and everything in between. When you discipline yourself to *what is,* you will stay the course.

7. **Discipline your disciplines.** Real freedom is not staged. It flows. It has its own rhythm. In this book, we've talked at length about the importance of **not** weighing yourself, **not** dieting, **not** setting up rigid rules, **not** buying expensive exercise equipment, and the list goes on. Unless you are careful with the rules you set up for yourself, you may feel there is little joy left for you, with all these *not*s cramping your style. I trust you'll **not** let this happen! This is a program about freedom, not bondage. That's why, eventually, you will want to bury your disciplines deep in your subconscious where they will work naturally *for* you, not against you.

In the beginning, you may need them to help your program of permanent weight loss take root. But then, bury them deep. Let them become artesian, instead of artificial, like the virtuoso who practices for years so that one day she may perform on stage as if she'd never practiced at all. When you discipline your disciplines, you will stay the course.

Kim's Story

For the remainder of this chapter, I want to give my pen and yellow pad over to a thirty-two-year-old woman whom I'll call Kim. I'm confident that Kim's story will encourage you, and make you say, "Hey, if Kim can do it, so can I." Here's Kim's story.

Twelve years after choosing to join the two percent who lose weight permanently, I have kept my weight off, have been liberated from past hurts, and have become what I know is an open, caring person who's really learned how to live. I suppose the most important principle I discovered at the outset was that the *whole-person* approach was not about food or weight. Instead, it was about dealing with my fears, guilt, and anger.

I still remember that day twelve years ago. I looked in the mirror, and I didn't like what I saw. I wanted desperately to look better. I was Miss Chubby. I would even buy clothes bigger than I needed, because I knew I'd fill them out eventually. One day I said, *That's it. I'm going to do this.* I sat down and wrote out what I wanted to look like, how I wanted to feel, the kinds of clothes I wanted to wear, along with a long list of the kinds of personality traits I'd like to have. Being friendly, positive, kind to others, serving people and God were just a few of my goals. I kept my list of objectives with me at all times and read it each night before I went to bed.

But I need to back up a bit with my story. My mother died when I was eleven, and her death devastated me. I have never known such depression of heart and mind. This new sound of loneliness shattered my already fragile world as I withdrew into a shell where there was only room for Kim. The trauma of losing my mother drove me toward a long, painful, intimate friendship with food.

"How are you holding up, Kim?" People would ask me.

"Oh, just fine. Doing great," I'd lie, torn up inside and wishing I could die. That was when I was in the sixth grade. My dad did what he could to raise me, and he gave me the best home he could. But I'd lost my mother and my friend. It did not go well with me for several years. Then, just three months before my high school graduation, my father died. I couldn't understand it. I was all alone, with no parents, no one really to understand me, and no real friends except the food that I'd adopted as my only means of survival. With the fear, hurt, and pain of my loss, I ate, and ate, and ate—and gained, and gained, and gained.

I remember walking into a Christian bookstore one evening, looking for a book on how to deal with loneliness, but all the salespersons were busy, so I just wandered around, looking for something on the shelves to get me through. I found nothing, so I just left, disappearing into the cold, rainy northwestern night.

Much of what happened during the next few months is a blur. I graduated from high school, worked part-time, and eventually started college. That's where I was motivated to start losing weight. But I've got to admit that part of my reason was because I wanted to look terrific for one really terrific guy. I loved him so much that I was determined to change. But it would not only be for him. Mainly, it would be for me. I was just tired of the pounds of blubber hanging down from my body, jiggling around like a tub of lard whenever I'd move.

I turned on the switch. *Okay, Kim, let's get going here.* Fortunately, I was exposed at that time to the *whole-person* approach, so I knew up front that my weight-loss program would not be about dieting, rigid exercise regimens, or diet pills. I'd been there, done that. None of it had worked. I can only describe my encounter with this new approach to weight loss as a beautiful, painful process. It wasn't always easy. In fact, it took me a long time to learn control and discipline. I even changed my traffic pattern for eating at school. I had always eaten in the school cafeteria where I could heap all the food I wanted on my plate three times a day—which I did, three times a day. Food was my friend, and I demanded a lot of intimacy. Now, with my new weight-loss program, I decided to go to the student union snack shop, where they would give me a pre-dished, sensible portion of food. I simply took what was offered. This *taking control* of my eating habits was one of the first things I learned to do. I was finally making healthy, prepared choices because *I* wanted to do it.

I found it awkward when I started to lose weight, because people would say, "Hey Kim, you on a diet or something?" Well, I *wasn't* on a diet, but how could I say, "No, I'm joining the two percent who lose weight permanently because they're dealing with the stuff in their lives, like guilt, fear, and anger, blah, blah, blah." They would be long gone before I'd finished my speech. So I learned to say, "No diet. I'm just cutting back." That felt good. *Just cutting back,* which was true.

I wish I could tell you it was all roses from then on. It wasn't. I don't know how many times I fell off the wagon. My greatest vice was sugar. I had been a sugaraholic ever since I could remember, and the urge for the sweet stuff never left me. I'd start with one piece of candy, and before long the whole box would be history. It was only when I remembered my long-term goals of how I wanted to look, feel, and be that I would drift back on course.

We "recovering heavy people" are terribly sensitive to criticism of any sort. Even if it's *not* criticism, we tend to read it into people's comments. Whenever anyone would call me chubby, or if I'd hear them talk behind my back, it crushed me. I'd say to myself, *Why are you so sensitive, Kim? They didn't mean it. Lighten up.* I'd try to talk myself into becoming a stronger person. Sometimes it worked. Lots of times it didn't. We who are heavy often run from relationships for fear of being hurt again. Or we compensate and take all the blame so we won't lose the people we think we love. It's a roller coaster, wild goose chase, chasing-a-greased-pig existence all rolled into one.

> I now know that a truly rich life depends on possibilities, and options, and opportunities to move from fear to hope, and from despair to joy.

Before I started losing weight *the right way,* I knew there was something missing in my weight-loss program, but I didn't know what it was. I did know that diets weren't working, because I'd been on enough of them. I said, *Kim, you're smart. Surely you can figure this all out. You just have some tools missing from your tool kit. Find out what you need, and go from there.* Self-talk really worked for me. In fact, this kind of ongoing discussion with myself often got me through the toughest times of my life. We who are heavy need help from wherever we can get it. We feel trapped in a body that we've become disgusted with—and that we know others are disgusted with also. I felt as if I'd been paralyzed in an accident after once being attractive and cool. I did not feel pretty at all when I was heavy. I now know that women with anorexia, who weigh next to nothing, often see themselves as having huge mounds of rolling flab hanging from their arms. They remain convinced they weigh much more than they actually do. So I know attractiveness is all a matter of perception.

Overweight people think that by becoming thin others will automatically like them, or they'll be happy, or they'll find overnight relational success. Not so. That's why it's not about food and weight. It's about what goes on inside that matters. Losing weight will not fix your life, and therein lies the rub. Most heavy people think, hope, and pray that if they can just get thin, the rest of their once dreary life will suddenly be sunrises and sunsets. This might be the sensational propaganda of the diet gurus and sellers of infomercial exercise equipment, but it doesn't hold up in the real world. Becoming thin does not make you happy in and of itself.

The two percent who lose weight permanently know how to stop and take stock of their lives. They work on the triggers that push them to binge on food. They know their assets and their liabilities. Most of all, they learn to be patient. That's what I had to learn, that it really is a matter of be-kind-to-yourself progress, and not perfection at any cost. Some people may criticize Richard Simmons for how he uses what they feel is a heightened level of excitement in his exercise programs and videos. But I want to come to his defense. It is Simmons' intimate understanding of compulsive overeaters that makes his work so moving. He understands that weight loss is something much greater and significant than just losing weight. His tears reflect an understanding of the deeper issues being touched as a result of the weight-loss process.

Little by little, I learned more about who I really was. Unconnected. Addicted to jewelry, nice clothes, cars, and other gadgets that shine and glitter. For a long time I didn't know what I needed to bring into my life to make me whole. If we who are overweight appear lost, it's because we are lost. Our behaviors are illogical and unpredictable. The world of disordered eating is a darkened universe that others do not understand. It's a world not based on logic or reason. If logic were the key, we'd all just go on diets, be thin, and be loved by everyone. The truth is that without coming to grips with our past, we will never stop abusing food. We just can't do it.

Guilt has no calories. Anger has no fat. Fear has no cholesterol. It's when we stuff these unresolved emotions into the already-cluttered basements of our minds that they become time bombs waiting to detonate who knows when. This was true for me. They were truly time bombs with short fuses, and they went off with painful regularity.

I want to close by saying this. I am at peace with myself today—with my body, my appearance, my personality, my relationships, and my work. I have developed the confidence to know that it's okay to communicate my needs. I have wonderful people in my life who respond to me and my needs in ways that help me feel safe. Safety, for me, is still a big word.

But most of all I'm at peace. I still have my share of conflicts and struggles, but my life now is about peace and contentment. I have lost my obsession for food because I have dealt with the real obsessions in my life. It's been twelve years since I lost those pounds. I never expect to see them again.

Kim's story is one of hundreds I've heard over the years. Like Goldilocks and the three bears looking for the right chair, millions of people continue to look for a weight-loss program that's just right for them. One size does not fit all. But when the whole person is addressed, our program of permanent weight loss leaves no one in the cold.

When you were in school, there were fewer As than Cs, but that didn't mean you weren't hoping for an A. That's why

I encourage you to model your life after the two percent who succeed, not the ninety-eight percent who fail to realize their goals.

A key reason the two percent lose weight permanently is that they've moved away from blaming themselves and others. An absence of blame, a willingness to take responsibility for their actions as adults, has changed their lives forever. Coupled with a passion for accountability, they are eager to be honest and trusting of others. People who are serious about losing weight permanently know it's not a time for Band-Aids, but rather for emotional surgery that gets to the heart of their deepest concerns.

What Are You Building?

A woman approached two stone masons working on a rather large project. She paused to ask each man, "What are you doing?" The first man looked at the woman and said hurriedly, "Lady, can't you see? I'm laying bricks!" She turned to the other workman and asked, "And what, may I ask, are you doing?" He paused for a moment, and with a faraway look in his eye said, "Madam, I'm building a beautiful cathedral which will shoot its spires high into the heavens, bringing glory to God for generations to come."

What are you doing? Laying bricks? Going through the motions of life, reliving past hurts, blaming others for your pain, and taking periodic guilt trips? Or are you building a landmark of beauty by becoming the person God created you to be? It is my prayer that the pages of this book have given you the blueprints to create such a building. If that is what I have given you with these pages, then that is the greatest gift an author could ever hope for. I wish you the best today, tomorrow, and forever as you enthusiastically join the two percent who lose weight permanently.

Action Plan #9

Putting It All Together

1. List at least five things you want to put into practice after reading this book. Then write out your personal action plan that will help make them become a reality for you.

   a. What I want to achieve:

   _____

   _____.

   My plan of action:

   _____

   _____.

   b. What I want to achieve:

   _____

   _____.

   My plan of action:

   _____

   _____.

   c. What I want to achieve:

   _____

   _____.

   My plan of action:

   _____

   _____.

d. What I want to achieve:

_____

_____.

My plan of action:

_____

_____.

e. What I want to achieve:

_____

_____.

My plan of action:

_____

_____.

2. In his best-selling book *Empires of the Mind,* Dr. Denis Waitley writes, "List the benefits of a new habit that would replace the old. Self-esteem, improved health, longevity, improved relationships, more professional productivity and respect, better focus, enhanced promotion potential, accelerated financial security . . . each helps lead to your ultimate goal of lifelong improvement and growth." Expand on Dr. Waitley's thoughts. Be specific on the immediate and long-range *benefits* that will come to you because you have chosen to lose weight permanently.

3. Finally, I would like you to write me a letter—either now or within the next month or so. Tell me about the progress you are making in your program to join the two percent who lose weight permanently. Tell me what you've learned, and whether I might have included other material or made certain things clearer in my writing to help you more. You can reach me at The

Center for Counseling & Health Resources, Inc. My address is in the back of the book. I look forward to hearing from you soon.

Theodore Roosevelt wrote, "Far better it is to dare mighty things, to win glorious triumphs, even though checkered by failure, than to take rank with those poor spirits who neither enjoy much nor suffer much, because they live in the gray twilight that knows not victory or defeat."

I hope you will dare to do those mighty things, regardless of the cost and despite the joyful pain they may bring at the start, that will be necessary to meet your objectives. Life on earth means there will be change. Growth, however, is optional. The choice is yours. God bless you and keep you for your commitment, daring, and never-ending courage as you endeavor to use the tools here to make your success last. It is my prayer that your attitude toward life in general—and your desire for permanent weight loss in particular—may be different for having read this book.

An ancient Hebrew prophet named Jeremiah knew bitterness, discouragement, and despair. His book was even called *Lamentations*. Yet from Jeremiah's position of grief and sadness, he was able to share a wisdom since confirmed by the ages. That same profound understanding of hope for a better future in the midst of pain can also help keep you moving deliberately, confidently, and inexorably toward your worthwhile goals. While this "weeping" prophet wrote of different events, different people, a different time, his words still provide men and women of today with great hope:

> "'For I know the plans I have for you,' declares the LORD, 'plans to prosper you and not to harm you, plans to give you hope and a future.'" (Jeremiah 29:11)

THE ADDICTION CHECKLIST

The following are some fairly common addictive personality traits. Check the ones that apply to you. The more you check, the more you will see an addictive pattern in your life. Record in a private journal or notebook as many examples as you can for each item checked. The result will be a descriptive picture of your total addictive tendencies. *Please talk these over with your counselor or support group.*

☐ I tend to conceal certain behaviors
☐ There is a slow deterioration of family "pride"
☐ I protect the consequences of my behavior
☐ I make secret pact(s) with other family members
☐ I tend to deny what is obvious to others
☐ I am feeling distant from other family members
☐ I am increasing my use of alibis, excuses, and justification for my actions
☐ There is a growing distrust within my family
☐ I engage in self-righteous criticism and tend to judge others
☐ I have more and more self-doubt and fear
☐ I often feel superior to others
☐ I neglect spiritual pursuits, including prayer and meditation
☐ I tend to overlook my own behavior
☐ I sense changes in eating or sleeping patterns

- [ ] I distrust those outside my family
- [ ] I'm having more accidents, illnesses, and injuries due to increased stress
- [ ] I often rationalize my behavior
- [ ] I find there's more loss of time on the job
- [ ] I often fantasize and obsess about my problems
- [ ] My ability to work or function is decreasing
- [ ] I hold the belief that if others changed, most of my problems would vanish
- [ ] I am having a conflict with my former value system—my once-clear set of personal ethics
- [ ] I attempt to "catch" or "trap" others in some act of which I do not approve
- [ ] I have made attempts at suicide or have nurtured suicidal thoughts
- [ ] My mood swings are intense, moving from high to low
- [ ] I have increasing financial problems
- [ ] I have a list of ongoing resentments and disappointments
- [ ] I feel I am over-extended and over-involved in my work and other outside activities
- [ ] I find myself losing friendships
- [ ] More and more I am engaging in self-defeating or degrading behavior

The alcoholic, workaholic, rageaholic, stimulusaholic, and foodaholic all incorporate their addictive behaviors into a life pattern that *seems* to work for them—a pattern their friends, colleagues, and family members are at their wits end to understand, much less accept. Drinking relaxes the drinker; overeating creates a sensation of fullness for the overeater; creating nonstop frantic, out-of-control conditions gives the stimulus-seeker an opportunity to *manage* his or her crisis, thus providing an opportunity for manipulation and control. It is management based on a negative premise, but it is nonetheless "management." What we are learning is that most of this kind of activity should not be given clinical labels. Many of these addictive personality traits are simply manifestations of obsessive-compulsive behavior, a problem that demands a different type of treatment and seldom requires medication.

APPENDIX TWO

ATTENTION DEFICIT DISORDER AND LEARNING DISABILITIES:
Their Relationship to Overeating

Much of this book emphasizes how we as individuals need to take responsibility for our behavior and stop blaming it on others—our parents, our jobs, our families. A recent trend, however, threatens to encourage people to blame their problems on Adult Attention Deficit Disorder or learning disabilities. Certainly people with these or other disorders will find life more challenging than those without these problems. However, these difficulties are no excuse for irresponsibility or inappropriate behavior. Shelley used them as an excuse.

Attention Deficit Disorder

Thirty-two-year-old Shelley had been a junior executive in an insurance firm for three and a half years. She had done well in her position, had lots of friends, and was slowly climbing the corporate ladder. When she started to have bouts of mild depression, she sought professional help. The diagnosis came back *manic-depression*, also known as bipolar disorder. She returned to work, but she was no longer the friendly, only occasionally depressed Shelley. "I am manic-depressive," she told her friends, "so don't be surprised if I'm in a funk for days at a time. It's also why I keep gaining weight. I have a medical problem, and I can't help myself."

As the situation became more tense at work, Shelley had increasing difficulty relating to her colleagues. A few months later Shelley announced that she now had been diagnosed as having Attention Deficit Disorder, a condition characterized by hyperactivity, distractibility, and low impulse control. She showed her coworkers her bottle of methylphenidate hydrochloride (Ritalin) which, she hoped, would correct the neurochemical imbalances in her brain. She asked her colleagues *please* to be aware of her deteriorating condition. According to Shelley, now that she had the diagnosis, she would no longer be able to be steady on the job. She also had a bonafide excuse why she could no longer be consistent with her exercise program. Her diagnosis was also why her once more-than-adequate communication skills suddenly became unpredictable, even sloppy. Sometimes she could work diligently until 10 P.M., while at other times she could barely plug along until closing time. She had been afflicted with certain physical challenges earlier, but now she had landed on a verifiable excuse for poor performance. She could blame it on Attention Deficit Disorder.

Her boss was skeptical at first. He saw mood swings and the occasional erratic behavior, but other than that Shelley seemed relatively healthy and stable, even though he observed compulsiveness with food and constant dieting.

Shelley defended herself and requested a large, private office instead of the smaller semi-private work area she'd had in the past. "I can't handle the noise anymore. It's just too distracting." Her doctor instructed her to make a list of the conditions she felt she needed to work more effectively—the kind of office enhancements that would relieve her from stress and distractions. Shelley was happy to oblige. It was amazing how much special equipment she suddenly needed. Her employer tried to accommodate her the best he could, defending the extra cost, saying, "This will be worth it, because when Shelley produces, she's terrific." But Shelley didn't produce.

The more perks Shelley received, the less work she accomplished and the more she complained about conditions in the office. Her demands continued to grow. She allowed no one to talk outside her office door, and there were to be no interruptions once the door was shut. "And please . . . hold my calls." But her productivity and efficiency continued to drop. Shelley always generated what seemed to be a legitimate excuse for not getting her work done. Exasperated, her employer finally had to let her go. Shelley claimed that she had been discriminated against because of her weight, her Attention Deficit Disorder, her manic-depression, and her other psychological and physical problems.

Once Shelley was diagnosed, she chose to use her conditions as excuses for unacceptable behavior. Meanwhile, her overeating and her compulsion for food remained a topic she refused to deal with honestly. Attention Deficit Disorder and manic-depression were the reasons she was not doing well. Deficits in her personality were the reasons she was forced to make food her friend. It wasn't her fault.

I am not saying Shelly did not have serious emotional challenges. What we know, however, is that compulsive overeaters may *appear* to manifest some of the symptoms of Attention Deficit Disorder without actually having the disorder. On many occasions, I have seen such a diagnosis used as a smokescreen for refusing to change behavior, give up an unhappy past, and join the two percent who lose weight permanently. The following questions indicate some of the tendencies of Adult Attention Deficit Disorder. Check the ones that are true for you.

☐ Do I ignore details?

☐ Do I often make careless mistakes?

☐ Is it hard for me to pay attention at home or at work?

☐ Do I fail to follow through on instructions?

☐ Do I fail to finish things I've started?

☐ Do I have difficulty in organizing tasks in a consistent manner?

☐ Do I tend to avoid activities that require sustained mental effort?

☐ Do I get distracted by extraneous noise?

☐ Am I forgetful in my daily activities?

☐ Do I have difficulty sitting still?

☐ Do I have feelings of physical restlessness?

☐ Do I have difficulty enjoying quiet, relaxing leisure activities?

☐ Do I feel I'm always "on the go," as if driven by a racing motor?

☐ Do I tend to talk excessively?

☐ Do I blurt out answers before the end of the question?

☐ Do I have difficulty waiting my turn?

☐ Do I often interrupt or intrude on others when they speak?

This is not a book on Attention Deficit Disorder or hyperactivity. However, we have observed that many of our patients often exhibit the above traits, mixed with elements of compulsive disorders. But they should not be given the clinical diagnosis of Attention Deficit/Hyperactivity Disorder. Similar symptoms can arise from:

- environmental toxins
- premature birth trauma
- excessive use of caffeine and sugar
- parenting styles
- learned impulsive behavior (learned in the home)
- TV and information overload

People who overeat and also believe they manifest some symptoms of Attention Deficit Disorder should carefully choose a fully licensed, qualified therapist or psychiatrist to do a full evaluation before accepting any labels. University of Washington faculty member Frederick Davis, M.D., told me he spends a lot of his time these days "undiagnosing" people who allegedly have Attention Deficit Disorder. We are not saying it doesn't exist. But if you have been diagnosed with Attention Deficit Disorder and have been told it is responsible for your weight problem, you need to be sure. Bring all the pieces of your life together in one place: the mental, physical, social, and spiritual.

The professionals you've seen to date may be so narrowly focused in their specialty that they have not seen the larger picture of *all* of who and what you are. I encourage you to seek counseling that includes behavior management, supportive problem solving, and new ways of dealing with key issues in your life.

Learning Disabilities

Learning disabilities are often tied to compulsive behaviors. I find that a high percentage of compulsive eaters have had great difficulty in school. Many have felt they completely failed academically, with their defeat starting as early as the fifth or sixth grade. We've documented that during those school years many seem to turn to food in a desperate, compulsive attempt to compensate for a poor performance in the classroom. But it did not work. Instead, they gave more ammunition to their classmates to use against them: "Hey, chubby, can't you read? Tubby, wanna do my homework for me, or are you too stupid?" This ridicule would lead to more compulsive eating, and a cycle was established. That is what happened to Michelle.

Throughout high school, especially during her senior year, Michelle was everything an honor student was not. Every class was a struggle: English, math, foreign language, science— even P.E. She could not remember when she was not in some special learning program during those difficult four years. However, while Michelle may have had an ugly academic record, there was nothing unattractive about her young body. She learned early the powers of seduction as she used her body and body language to tantalize and manipulate the boys in her school. She was slender and beautiful and quickly became accomplished in compensating for her academic failures by acquiring sexual favors.

Promiscuity was the only way she knew how to cope with her sense of failure. As an adult, her compulsive behaviors increased. When she wanted acceptance as an adult, she'd go to parties and demand all the attention by throwing herself at men. By the time she married, she had a huge reservoir of poisonous compulsivity. With an increasingly high need for emotional stimulation, Michelle kept turning to food for comfort, a condition that latter became full-blown bulimia. She also became a compulsive spender and a rageaholic, known for uncontrollable mood swings. She and her new husband ended up in counseling early in their marriage. But Michelle's cravings for sex continued, including two affairs with her husband's friends which pushed the marriage off the deep end.

Michelle could never get enough of anything to be happy. Her family physician misdiagnosed her as manic-depressive, which she appeared to be on the surface. However, someone who knew her history would have seen that it was her learning disabilities coupled with numerous life failures that encouraged her to seek her own pain-killing remedies to ease her distress.

People who lose weight permanently recognize the existence of personality influences such as Attention Deficit Disorder and learning disabilities. But they do not permit these personality influences to be excuses for irresponsible behavior. In fact, when they come face to face with their compulsive behavior, many will say as one woman did, "When I finally dealt with the root of my compulsive behaviors, my personality defects (Attention Deficit Disorder and learning disabilities) began to diminish in my life, at least to the point where I could control them. I still found learning and concentration difficult, but I learned to live with it and no longer used my problems as an excuse to stay fat. I still wanted to be compulsive at times, but I knew I finally had the option of making a healthy choice. And that was the point: the choice was mine."

For those with properly diagnosed Attention Deficit Disorder or learning disabilities, the whole-person approach to permanent weight loss has been effective. They learn that:

1. **Long-term goals can be reached.** They have always had difficulty in reaching long-term goals, permanent weight loss included. But they find they *can* reach their goals when they address the *whole person* and deal with all their issues, not just weight. They reprogram themselves to think long-term. To set goals will always be frustrating, and for many it will never get any easier. But they learn they are neither hopeless nor helpless.

2. **Slowing down and thinking before acting** makes them more aware of the consequences of their behavior. Their pattern has often been to speak first and think sometime later, ignoring the consequences of this behavior. They have to adjust their internal clocks to a slower speed, recognizing that it's less wear and tear on their bodies if they *ease on down the road.* Among the wonderful, positive consequences of thinking before acting is less hyperactivity and a deep sense of living a productive, effective life.

3. **They can be more understanding and sensitive to others.** They once had zero tolerance for themselves

and others. But they now espouse what one of my patients calls "The Eleventh Commandment: Blessed are the flexible, for they shall not break." They discover that people begin to enjoy their company when they are more tolerant of others. They begin thinking of the needs of others, and as they do, they begin to lose weight.

4. **They find it helpful to be held accountable to others.** People with negative personality influences who succeed in weight loss do so by moving from rigid, compulsive coping (usually diet-promoted) to living with progress, not perfection. They recognize the need for accountability which places the onus on them to be honest with themselves and others. Those with Attention Deficit Disorder and other learning disabilities learn to become open to new information. They encourage feedback and begin realizing they are not alone in this world. They really do have friends.

RAISING CHILDREN TO RESIST EATING PROBLEMS

What about our children? We now know that almost a fourth of all children in the United States are overweight. The unfortunate prediction is that in most cases these children will grow up to become overweight adults, who will have overweight children, who will have overweight—even obese—offspring. What causes this inappropriate friendship with food? Of course, the media share some responsibility for the way food and beauty are dealt with in commercials and regular programming. But we also see that overeating tends to run in families. So, what can parents do to help their children avoid the trap of using food as a friend? Here are five things a child needs to grow up with a healthy attitude toward herself and food:

Honesty. When you make promises, keep them. Be a person of your word so that your child is not constantly dealing with disappointments.

Affection. Every child needs affection, including hugs, verbal statements of love, and unrushed attention. Children who know they are valued are less likely to turn to food for comfort.

Safety. Teach your child to seek out people who are safe—emotionally, physically and sexually. Shout this message loud and clear to your children. Protect your child from emotional and physical harm and help him learn how to protect himself as he grows older.

Boundaries. Let your child know how important boundaries are for you. It's okay to draw a line in the emotional sand. As your child grows, she will also learn where the boundaries are and how to keep them. This will give her resilience and make her unlikely to be a victim.

Structure. Children need structure. One child, playing on the school playground, was heard complaining to his teacher, "Do we really have to do what we want to today?" I continue to hear adults cry out for the same kind of direction. We all need structure, appropriate traditions, and a sense that some things are going to be the same day after day.

What you learned as a child may not have prepared you to live a happy, effective life. You can change that for your own children, however, if you help them learn how to make their own happiness. The following is a list of platitudes that many children hear and end up following. But they are not healthy directions for living. Try to avoid giving your children these messages:

- Always look as if you have it all together.
- Be brave (and hide your true feelings).
- Always put others first and yourself last.
- Do not cry, even when you are crying inside.
- Clean your plate because there are starving people in China . . . Africa . . . India, etc.
- Never let anyone see you make a mistake.
- Never make a mess.
- Help others but ignore your own needs.

If you are pawning these ideas off on yourself or your children, please take a good look at the message you are conveying. As you learn to take the risk of appreciating who you are, help your child do the same. The greatest gift you can give your child is the encouragement to become the person God intended him or her to be.

In *Parenthood without Hassles, Well, Almost!* Dr. Kevin Leman, who is also the author of *Making Children Mind without Losing Yours,* gives us a marvelous summary of what children need. I would like to see it posted on the refrigerator of every American home:

A Child's Ten Commandments to Parents

1. My hands are small; please don't expect perfection whenever I make a bed, draw a picture, or throw a ball. My legs are short; please slow down so that I can keep up with you.
2. My eyes have not seen the world as yours have; please let me explore safely: Don't restrict me unnecessarily.
3. Housework will always be there. I'm only little for such a short time—please take time to explain things to me about this wonderful world, and do so willingly.
4. My feelings are tender; please treasure me as God intended you to do, holding me accountable for my actions, giving me guidelines to live by, and disciplining me in a loving manner.
5. I am a special gift from God; please treasure me as God intended you to do, holding me accountable for my actions, giving me guidelines to live by, and disciplining me in a loving manner.
6. I need your encouragement, but not your praise, to grow. Please go easy on the criticism; remember, you can criticize the things I do without criticizing me.
7. Please give me the freedom to make decisions concerning myself. Permit me to fail so I can learn from my mistakes.

8. Please don't do things over for me. Somehow that makes me feel that my efforts didn't quite measure up to your expectations.

9. Please don't be afraid to leave for a weekend together. Kids need vacations from parents, just as parents need vacations from kids. Besides, it's a great way to show us kids that your marriage is very special.

10. Please take me to Sunday school and church regularly, setting a good example for me to follow. I enjoy learning more about God.

ABOUT THE AUTHOR

Gregory L. Jantz, who holds a doctoral degree in counseling and health psychology, is the executive director of The Center for Counseling and Health Resources, Inc., headquartered in Edmonds, Washington. The Center is known to individuals in the Northwest—and now around the world—as "a place of hope." He and his wife, LaFon, direct a diverse offering of treatment programs in Washington state.

In addition, Dr. Jantz has developed a line of eating disorder formulas, called *CenterLine,* to aid clients in supporting physical well-being unique to eating disorders and food addictions. He is author of two other books: *Hope, Help, & Healing for Eating Disorders* and *Healing the Scars of Emotional Abuse* (available through The Center or your local bookstore).

Dr. Jantz first began work with eating disorders while an intern in a women's prison. However, his search to find answers and help for the women he counseled was often met with more questions than solutions. Integrating his training in psychology and nutrition, Dr. Jantz developed a method of treatment he calls *the whole-person approach,* which takes into account not just the emotional health of the individual but also the physical, relational, and spiritual state of the person affected by an eating disorder.

Losing Weight Permanently is a classic example of Dr. Jantz's effective, hope-filled approach to helping people find true and lasting health and wholeness.

For more information about treatment, telecounseling, radio/TV interviews, national seminars, or hosting an event with Dr. Jantz in your community, please call or write:

Director of Seminars
The Center for Counseling and Health Resources, Inc.
P.O. Box 700
Edmonds, WA 98020
Phone: (206) 771-5166
Fax: (206) 670-2807
E-mail: THECENTERINC.MSN.COM
The Internet (for specific information and counseling):
   http://www3.imall.com/the_center/

For information on specialized eating disorder nutritional formulas or to receive an order form, call:

Eating Disorder Order Department
The Center for Counseling and Health Resources, Inc.
Phone: (206) 771-5166
Fax: (206) 670-2807
E-mail: THECENTERINC.MSN.COM